The Feminist Lie

Bob Lewis

Copyright © 2017 Bob Lewis

All rights reserved.

ISBN: 1546926097
ISBN-13: 9781546926092

This Book Is Dedicated To:

The victims,

The honorable men abused and discarded;

The victims of false rape and domestic violence allegations;

Those who've had their lives destroyed

or been wrongfully imprisoned;

The male victims of rape and domestic assault;

The women harmed by feminist ideology

CONTENTS

	Acknowledgments	i
	Introduction	iii
1	Feminism and Tactics	1
2	History Feminists Ignore	Pg 12
3	Patriarchy & Male Privilege	Pg 38
4	The Wage Gap Lie	Pg 67
5	The False Rape Pandemic	Pg 75
6	Debunking the DV Lies	Pg 104
7	Female Privilege	Pg 130
8	Feminism Harms Women	Pg 148
9	Feminism's Reaction	Pg 165
10	The Solutions	Pg 179
	About the Author	Pg 186

ACKNOWLEDGMENTS

Even though I'm the author, the creation of this work was a collaborative effort.

This text wouldn't have been possible without the extensive scientific research, investigative journalism, and courage of the many professionals I cited throughout my writing.

Just as important, if not more so, are the independent journalists and online content creators, whether they're video creators, vloggers, or bloggers. This also includes the shit posters, meme creators, and online trolls. Society owes these independent online voices our most sincere gratitude because even though feminism was able to effectively silence, intimidate, or otherwise suppress the many traditional and academic voices of opposition, opposition online stood firm.

Today, these online voices still stand as vanguards against constant onslaught from Feminists. They've been so effective in countering the feminist narrative that they've changed the conversation. Feminists know their days are numbered, which is why they're making constant calls to silence voices of opposition by maliciously reframing disagreement as a hate crime.

With that said, it's just as important to thank the feminists I cite here also. You see, without their hypocrisy and man-hating bigotry, this book and other voices of reason and feminist opposition wouldn't be necessary.

Also, I'd like to thank the everyone who supported me during the last stages of writing this book: Turd Flinging

Monkey, FeedinDaCat, the Monkey Business Discord crew, and the beta readers.

A huge thank you to Miasman for the many hours he spent suffering through drafts, editing, and providing indispensible feedback. It made all the difference.

Finally, I'd like to thank my youngest son and my son-in-law for their unwavering support.

This book exists because of all of you.

INTRODUCTION

"Without data, you're just another person with an opinion"
                                            -W. Edwards Deming

As far as I can tell, the book on your screen or holding in your hands is the first of its kind. While there are many voices that oppose feminism, there are few books that criticize feminism at the level it deserves. To my knowledge, feminism has never been called to account for the damage its ideology continues to cause to families, communities, and Western society. Nor has any book, before this one, ever described in brutal detail how it discriminates against men and harms women.

While I wrote with sarcasm and irreverence, it was solely to soften the harsh realities contained herein. This book is a sobering true story of tragedy, suicide, and murder directly caused by feminism. It not only chronicles true stories that show feminism's discrimination against men, it's backed by peer-reviewed research. Additionally, it includes investigative journalism that proves feminism was never about equality. The reality is that feminism doesn't just victimize men. It also victimizes women, children, families, and communities.

There were many times while researching and writing this book I had to step away and hold back tears. Don't be surprised if you experience something similar.

While each chapter can be read independently, reading the book from start to finish will give far greater insight.

Whether you're a completely ignorant "normie" or a red-pilled veteran, the knowledge contained herein will better prepare and educate you about the dangers of feminism.

When you're finished reading this book and you enjoyed it or learned something from it, I'd be honored if you'd told others about it through social media, face-to-face interactions, or by writing a review online. As a first-time self-published author, the hardest part of the process is letting the world know a book like this exists. Thank you for your purchase.

1. FEMINISM AND TACTICS

Before we can have a credible discussion about feminist lies and hypocrisies, we should first briefly discuss the role propaganda plays in spreading ideology, whether it's the ideology of feminism, white supremacy, or any other movement.

What's propaganda? For purposes of this book, I'm using the following definitions:

The Merriam-Webster dictionary defines propaganda as,

> "...the spreading of ideas, information, or rumor for the purpose of helping or injuring an institution, a cause, or a person...ideas, facts, or allegations spread deliberately to further one's cause or to damage an opposing cause; also : a public action having such an effect."

The Oxford online dictionary defines propaganda as,

> *"Information, especially of a biased or misleading nature, used to promote a political cause or point of view."*

Throughout history, there's never been a political issue discussed in the public square that's been free from propaganda. Technically speaking, this book is a form of propaganda, based on the above definitions. I'm using this book to spread the facts and debunk the lies about feminist ideology while providing commentary to educate and empower those who oppose the misguided hypocrisy feminist ideology advocates.

With that said, no conversation on feminism can be complete without consideration of the role gynocentrism plays within feminist ideology. Merriam-Webster concisely defines gynocentrism as,

> *"dominated by or emphasizing feminine interests or a feminine point of view."*

The Urban Dictionary further defines gynocentrism and provides an example of its usage within the definition itself,

> *"Always putting the woman first even if it is to the detriment of others. Often results in female supremacy.*
>
> *Man 1 - You should always pay your woman's bills.*
>
> *Man 2 - But aren't men and women equal? Shouldn't she pay her own bills?*
>
> *Man 1 - Oh, yes, that was stupid of me. The gynocentrism in our culture prevents me from thinking logically at times. I apologize."*

Finally, we need to define Misandry. Misandry plays an integral role in feminism and feminist ideology cannot survive without it. Merriam-Webster defines it simply as,

> *"A hatred of men."*

With these definitions out of the way, we're now ready to delve into the rabbit hole of hate created by feminism.

At its most basic level, feminism began as a rebellion against marriage and family values. Early feminists believed that once married, a woman's identity disappeared. To gain sympathy, many early feminists reframed the institution of marriage as a form of slavery. To support their view, they pointed out that women didn't have many of the rights society given to men. While on the surface this appears to be a completely legitimate complaint. Upon closer inspection, it completely falls apart.

While these early feminists were correct in their observation that women didn't have the rights given to men, they completely ignored the other side of the coin. Women also didn't bear any of the responsibilities that their male counterparts held. Feminists ignored something men have known for thousands of years. Rights are earned based on responsibilities. Simply put, the more responsibility a person accepts, the more rights they're able to earn.

Women weren't required to defend their lands in times of war. Women weren't required to work. They could rely on their husbands for 100% of their financial support. Women weren't required to do anything, other than birth and raise children and keep their family homes in order. Outside of this, their husbands took responsibility for everything else.

Today, at its core, feminist ideology is little changed. It's still antagonistic to marriage and family values and feminists still agitate for rights and privileges free from responsibility.

While there are many subsets and generations (also known as waves) of feminism, for purposes of this book, we'll only be briefly identifying two of them, choice feminism and intersectional feminism. The main reason I'm limiting my discussion to these two exclusively is because all other types of feminism fall within one of these two categories, in some form.

Choice feminism is sometimes referred to as individual feminism. In general terms, this brand of feminism promotes the personal choices a woman makes and her individual liberties, over what is good of the feminist group. To reiterate, this brand of feminism advocated that any choice the individual woman makes is acceptable as long as she is free to choose it. Under this ideology, it's just as acceptable to be a sex worker, or a single mother, as it is to be a full-time career woman. It's also the brand of feminism that's most often advocated by female celebrities and is strongly supported by many first and second wave feminists.

Intersectional feminism was first coined in 1989 by Kimberle Crenshaw. This brand of feminism seeks to incorporate feminism to the civil rights movement by creating a type of hierarchy of oppression olympics where some feminists are more oppressed than others based on their gender, race or ethnicity, class, and ability (or disability). Thus a black male feminist may be considered more oppressed than a rich white female feminist, especially if that black male feminist is disabled. Further, the more oppressed a feminist is perceived on the oppression olympic scale, the more valuable she is to the intersectional feminist movement.

Intersectional feminists strongly oppose choice feminism and they seek to control women as a group, as opposed to allowing each woman the freedom to choose their own path in life. This brand of feminism often openly incorporates communist, socialist, and Marxist ideologies its teachings and messaging. They also believe that feminists cannot be oppressors. This belief is conveniently used to excuse their own bigotry, oppression, and misandry. To be clear, they use this as an excuse to justify violence against anyone...even other women...who disagree with their ideologies.

Intersectional feminists successfully co-opted civil rights activism to form the foundations of the social justice movement. As a result, their bigotry, racism against whites, and overall misandry set civil rights back at least 50 years.

Regardless of their differences, both brands of feminism believe in the conspiracy theory that a cabal of men is responsible for what feminists perceive to be a systemic oppression of women. They refer to this cabal as the "patriarchy." They use their opposition to this mythical patriarchy as justification for every feminist act, even though there's never been any objective evidence that such an oppressive gender-based cabal exists anywhere in history outside of Islam.

Now that we have a very general primer on the two main feminist ideologies, let's discuss the propaganda and debate tactics that feminists use.

While I could get into every single propaganda tactic feminists use, this subject is a large enough body of knowledge that it warrants its own book. Therefore, I'll briefly highlight some of the more common tactics that feminists use to gain support while silencing their critics.

We'll start with entryism. The Oxford Living Dictionary defines entryism as,

> "*The infiltration of a political party by members of another group, with the intention of subverting its policies or objectives.*"

While far from a new concept, feminists often use this tactic to gain membership into groups under false pretenses in order to usurp control from within and repurpose these groups to advocate feminist ideologies. Entryism was first advocated in 1934 by Trotsky as part of his writings on the "*French Turn*" in order to co-opt other organizations and spread Leninism.

In Feminism, one prominent feminist who's very successfully used this tactic is Anita Sarkeesian. She's a video game commentator and political activist. Publicly, she claims to be a lifelong video game fan who realized through playing video games that many games were sexist. Sarkeesian used this narrative to gain acceptance and credibility within the gaming community. It provided her a platform to spread her extreme brand of intersectional feminist ideology. Her beliefs are so extreme, that Sarkeesian's even on video proclaiming everything's sexist and everything is misogynist, even if it's not. Make no mistake, Sarkeesian's a fanatic.

However, after Sarkeesian gained near-instant popularity, a video surfaced from 2011. She was giving a lecture to college students and openly admitted she wasn't a fan of video games. She goes on to admit she learned to play video games and involved herself in the video game community for the express purpose of spreading feminism.

In her words,

> *"I'm not a fan of video games. I actually had to learn a lot about video games in the process of making this."*

Sarkeesian's entire career as a feminist video game commentator is based on the lie that she was a long time video game fan. This was a lie she continuously retold to the video gaming community and others to falsely establish credibility and gain access to the highest levels of the video gaming and the tech industry establishments. In fact, this lie was so completely believed she was invited to the United Nations to speak in support of internet censorship of anti-feminist messages and criticisms.

We also see many examples of feminists employing unethical entryist tactics like this in almost every industry and in all Western governments. They've infiltrated sports, education, and health care, to name but a few. In fact, feminists have formed their own vast global network of private and public organizations for the express purpose of creating and maintaining government policies that support the feminist ideology. A few examples of these organizations include the League of Women Voters and the National Organization of Women. These organizations don't just promote feminist ideologies, they promote and fund feminist candidates to government office while funding attacks against their preferred candidate's opponents.

This ideological man-hating spider-webbed network is largely responsible for some of the most gynocentric laws and legal systems in the Western world...from gender-biased family courts to federal VAWA (Violence Against Women Act) laws that only protect women while painting all men as criminals. Some of the major policy and social consequences of these efforts will be addressed in later chapters.

When spreading their propaganda or when confronted with their hypocrisy, feminists use a variety of unethical and intellectually dishonest debate techniques to defend their ideology. You will often be unable to counter feminist arguments until you're able to identify these unethical tactics. However, even if you counter them, feminist allies may still attack you for your disagreement. They do this by reframing disagreement as hate speech.

With that in mind, I'll very briefly describe the most common tactics feminists use to better prepare you to defend yourself when you're confronted by feminist hypocrisy.

Note, feminists often will preemptively use these debate tactics to silence any legitimate opposition and criticism before any meaningful discussion about the real issues can ever take place. To me, feminists that do this are practicing a form of censorship and intellectual dishonesty.

Perhaps the most common tactic employed by feminists is deflection. This is one of the "go to" argument techniques used by feminists. I believe the Urban Dictionary has one of the most concise and correct definitions of deflection under their definition of "deflective arguing," quoted in pertinent part,

> *"This is when somebody argues by deflecting anything said against them.*
>
> *They will never address any issues brought against them or their point but will instantly bring something else up to change the subject*
>
> *People do this because they know damn well*

> *if they try to address the issue or stay relevant to it, there entire argument will get derailed"*

For example, if you point out a prominent feminist who's voiced a sexist hatred of men, feminists won't criticize that feminist, nor will they disavow that feminist's man-hating statements, rather, they'll tell you, *"not all feminists are like that."* Just as commonly, they'll respond with, *"she isn't a real feminist."*

Neither of these arguments addresses the sexist misandrist statement made or the man-hating feminist who made them. They're designed to deflect attention from the bigotry because feminists know these statements represent an indefensible hypocrisy within their movement.

This leads us to our second extremely common feminist debate tactic, personal attacks and shaming. The beauty of personal attacks is that they're only used when no valid argument exists. To me, they're an admission of defeat. While a tactic in and of itself, a personal attack or shaming is just another form of deflection to avoid addressing any valid criticism. When feminist hypocrisy and ideology is questioned, rather than respond to the issues, feminists will, more often than not, attack the critic. They usually do this by proclaiming that the speaker is a *"bitter"* man who *"cannot get a girlfriend."* There are many other examples of feminists using these types of personal attacks elsewhere, so I won't spend any more time on them here.

Another common tactic feminists use is reframing and false comparisons (also known as false dichotomies). Technically, these are two separate tactics. However, they're so similar and complimentary that they almost completely overlap and feminists often use them together. Feminists often bounce from one to another as necessary as another type of deflection to keep critics off-balance.

An example of when reframing happens is when men speak of gender equality in the context of men's rights. Anytime men's rights or men's equality is brought up, feminists will reframe any support for men's equality as misogyny. If men are denied their due process rights after being falsely accused of rape and speak out against it, they're reframed as rape apologists.

Feminists often use false comparisons to create support for their position where none exists. For example: feminists state that if a person believes in equal rights, then by definition, they're also a feminist. However, this couldn't be further from the truth. Feminists advocate gynocentrism, not gender equality. After listening to feminists speak on their beliefs, this is very easy to perceive.

Both tactics are used to silence opposition while avoiding any legitimate discussion of any of the valid issues raised by critics of feminist ideology.

If their goal was gender equality, why do feminists use such unethical propaganda tactics to silence their critics? It's because feminism isn't really about equality, it's about female superiority.

Finally, the last major debate technique feminists use is creating a public scene.

This is one of the most effective and at the same time, one of the most unethical techniques in a feminist's debate arsenal. What they do is lure their opponent into a crowd or public arena where they have allies hiding in the crowd. Then if their opponent actually starts making valid points and the crowd starts turning on the feminist, she will actually have a meltdown. Once her allies see this, they too will meltdown and become both belligerent and disruptive. Then, they will often falsely accuse the feminist's opponent of sexism, assault, harassment or any other crime they can use to gain sympathy. Afterward, they will wage a public relations campaign to further enhance their false narrative while disparaging the person who dared disagree with them. While there are many examples of this on social media and online videos. The mainstream media usually only reports the false narrative feminists create.

The reality is that there are only two debate tactics that are effective in dealing with feminist hypocrisy. They're logic and facts.

If you rely on indisputable facts and objective logic, you will often prevail in any debate of feminist ideology. You'll know you've won when they attempt to censor your message and refuse to address anything you have to say.

However, even if you win a debate with a feminist, they're so fanatical they'll never concede they're wrong.

2 HISTORY FEMINISTS IGNORE

This chapter is divided into two parts. First, I'll highlight some successful powerful women in history. Then the second part will contrast these strong independently successful women with information about historically significant feminists.

With that in mind, let's begin.

Everywhere in the media, we're repeatedly told by feminists that if the feminist movement didn't exist, women wouldn't have any of the rights and privileges they have today. Their reason, as discussed in the earlier chapter, is that because of a long-standing patriarchal system of male oppression, women were prevented from reaching their full potential in educational, financial, and academic achievement.

The reality, however, demonstrates this to be simply untrue.

What follows are highlights of history that feminists,

almost universally, ignore. They ignore them because they completely debunk their false narrative of unilateral patriarchal oppression of women throughout history. As you will see, even before the United States was conceived and founded, women had many rights equal to men and achieved levels of prominence equal to and often exceeding the men surrounding them. Privilege and oppression weren't based on gender, but rather wealth and the corresponding power that came with it.

While history has too many examples of powerful women to include here, I've included some highlights to prove how verifiably dishonest feminists continue to be about their false narrative of oppression.

Our first example is from Africa, one of the most prominent ancient rulers was the Egyptian queen Cleopatra. In fact, there were seven queens of Egypt named Cleopatra. If there was a patriarchy, none of these queens could've ever been the supreme ruler of Egypt. More importantly, but also ignored by feminists, is that Egypt was known for many queens other than the seven Cleopatras. Queen Hatshepsut was the fifth Pharaoh of the eighteenth dynasty of Egypt who took the throne in 1478 BC. While Queen Tiye ruled together with her husband, she was so wise and respected, many foreign dignitaries dealt with her directly and exclusively, rather than her husband. Nefertiti, another woman was also an Egyptian queen who, after her husband died, ruled Egypt. The first confirmed queen to rule Egypt was Sobekneferu, who ruled in the twelfth dynasty. However, even before then, there were at least six other queens mentioned in the history books.

The reality is that across the African continent, there's evidence of dozens of female rulers. Many of them owned slaves.

According to the Catholic Encyclopedia published in 1913, a Spanish woman Julianna Morell, born on February 16, 1594, started studying Greek, Latin, and Hebrew when she was only four years old. She is later documented as studying physics, metaphysics, religious canon, and civil law. Julianna obtained her doctorate of law in 1608. She was just 14 years old.

Had there been a male patriarchy that oppressed women, Julianna would've never been allowed to thrive and obtain the level of academic success she did. The reality is that she wasn't oppressed. Like anyone else successful in life, she worked hard and was rewarded for her efforts.

For the sake of brevity, I'll only mention Joan of Arc by name and mention the many queens throughout history that ruled various countries in Europe. If you'd like to find out more about these powerful female monarchs, I'm confident in your ability to conduct an internet search on European history.

In the Americas in 1639, an all-female school, the L'Ecole des Ursulines de Quebec, located in what is now the State of Maine, focused exclusively on educating girls. Boys weren't allowed. Yet, we always hear feminists complain about how the patriarchy has held them back in education. This all women's college is still in operation at the time of this writing. Clearly, no Patriarchy prevented this all women's school from being successful for almost 400 years.

On October 4, 1639, Margaret Brent became the first documented female land owner in the Americas. Initially she received about 70 acres of land, though later she and her sister had their land grant enlarged to 800 acres each. The Governor of the Maryland colony, Lord Calvert, trusted and respected her so much that he appointed her as the executrix of his estate in 1647. Clearly not only were women landowners and holders of leadership positions in society prior to first wave feminism, but this is just one more example that thoroughly debunks the feminist lie of being historically oppressed. Yet, to hear feminists tell it, male oppression of women made it impossible to obtain this level of success.

According to the National Women's History Museum, Oberlin college, located in Oberlin, Ohio, was admitting women as early as 1833. The first woman to achieve a bachelor's degree, according to US News, was Catherine Brewer. She graduated from Wesleyan College on July 16, 1840, in Macon, Georgia. In 1849, Elizabeth Blackwell was the first woman to graduate from Geneva Medical School in Geneva, New York. She's also notable because she graduated at the top of her class. In 1862, Mary Jane Patterson, an African-American woman, got her bachelor's degree from Oberlin College. In 1866, Lucy Hobbs got her D.D.S. from Ohio College of Dental Surgery to become the first female dental surgeon in the United States.

Ada Kepley graduated from law school at the Union College of Law in Chicago, Illinois in 1870. Helen Magill became the first American woman to receive her Ph.D in 1877. She majored in Greek Studies at Boston University.

In the United States even before 1900, women attended and graduated college, just like men.

These highlights represent only a small fraction of the women throughout history who have achieved academic, social, or governmental success equal to or greater than their male contemporaries. These are the facts in history feminists don't want you to know.

Now let's look at a few prominent women feminists hold as icons of their ideology.

Whenever feminists talk about their history, they always talk about how they're the champions for equality from equal pay, voting rights, racial equality, and of course, gender equality. To hear feminists frame it, you'd think that they are courageous heroes who always approach the issues from the moral high ground. Unfortunately, this is a gross misrepresentation and revisionist history.

It turns out that most feminists throughout history were raging bigots and misandrists (man-haters). These early feminists made no efforts to hide their racism and other aspects of their bigotry. So, while modern feminists claim these historical figures advocated equality, they didn't. They advocated gynocentrism. In some cases, as you will see, they even advocated genocide.

Lets' start with Mary Wollestonecraft, a British woman widely considered to be the grandmother of British feminism. In 1792, she published one of the first books on feminism called: "*A Vindication of the Rights of Woman.*" In her book, Wollestonecraft advocates for more social and moral equality between the sexes, similar to egalitarianism.

What's interesting about her book is Wollestonecraft's criticism of women.

Wollestonecraft says women have acquired all the follies and vices of civilization and missed the "*useful fruit.*" She continues her scathing criticism of women stating their emotions are so inflamed that they're controlled by their feelings. She then posits that women's focus on feelings over facts renders them not only uncomfortable themselves, but also troublesome to others. She goes on to criticize women for focusing on things that emotionally excite their feelings to the point of instability. To Wollestonecraft, this causes women to waver in their convictions and pursuits, not because of any valid reason, but because women experience contradictory emotions and are subject to fleeting passions. She goes on to conclude that women cultivate their mind for the express purpose of inflaming their passions, which doesn't make them strong women, but rather, leads them to, *"a mixture of madness and folly!"*

Remember, these were the words of the grandmother of the feminist movement. They weren't coming from a misogynistic men's rights activist. Ironically, the criticisms Wollestonecraft leveled at women in 1792 mirror the same critiques of feminism over two hundred years later in 2017.

When Wollestonecraft died at 38 years old, her husband, William Godwin, wrote a biography about her. He disclosed her love affairs, an illegitimate child, and her mental instability that led to her attempting suicide multiple times. Clearly, Wollestonecraft's criticism of women had some basis in personal experience.

Elizabeth Cady Stanton was an American leader in the early women's rights movement and was a close associate of Susan B. Anthony, another prominent feminist, featured on the American dollar coin. In 1868, Stanton gave a speech at the Women's Suffrage Convention in Washington DC. In the very beginning of her speech, which was documented, she states,

> *"The male element is a destructive force, stern, selfish, aggrandizing, loving war, violence, conquest, acquisition, breeding in the material and moral world alike discord, disorder, disease, and death."*

Had there been a patriarchy oppressing women at the time, she wouldn't have been able to give a speech in Washington DC. Even further, the Woman's Suffrage Convention wouldn't have existed. Toward the end of her speech, she states she doesn't feel this way about all men, only some of them. However, three decades later, she admitted her true feelings about men. On December 27, 1890. Thirty years later, she wrote in her diary,

> *"We are, as a sex, infinitely superior to men."*

Clearly, she didn't believe in equality, but rather feminist supremacy, gynocentrism.

Further, both she and Anthony openly admitted their racism. Even though Anthony and Stanton both worked with Abolitionists, when it came time to support the African-American right to vote, both opposed it. There are multiple accounts of their racism documented elsewhere so I won't elaborate those examples here.

Racism was very common among early feminists. These women weren't the outliers.

With that in mind, no study of feminist history can be complete without an objective consideration of how the American eugenics movement inspired both feminist ideology and the Nazi Jewish genocide which ultimately murdered tens of thousands of Germans and millions of Jews.

The term, eugenics, was first coined in 1883 by its founder, Englishman Francis Galton in his book, *"Inquiries Into Human Faculty and Development."*

Merriam Webster defines eugenics as,

> *"a science that deals with the improvement*

of hereditary quality of a race or breed."

Eugenics proposed these racial improvements by controlling human breeding patterns and other forms of population control, that included the removal of those who eugenicists felt unfit.

Racist elites and academics in the United States almost immediately fell in love with eugenics. Backed by their funding and support, it took the nation by storm. Funding was provided by the Carnegie Institution, Rockefeller Foundation, the Harriman Railroad Fortune and many others.

In 1903, the American Breeders Association, one of the first eugenics organizations in the United States, had their initial meeting in St. Louis, Missouri. This meeting was the first of its kind and marked a transition point within the movement.

In 1910, prominent eugenicist Charles B. Davenport formed the Eugenics Record Office. By the 1920s, Davenport and his organization became one of the prominent leaders of the American eugenics movement. Davenport's organization collected genealogical lists of families across the country which they used to target entire family lines he and his associates deemed unfit for society.

In 1912, the First International Eugenics Congress held at the University of London. At that event, the American Breeders Association presented their eugenics committee's preliminary report. This committee featured prominent doctors, judges, lawyers, and academics from such institutions as Princeton, Johns Hopkins, Harvard, Cornell, Yale and even government institutions such as the U.S. Bureau of Statistics.

In their report, the American Breeder's Association stated their purpose was to stand against what they perceived as an increase in the number of, "*defective classes.*" They identified these people as morally retarded and a burden on society. They defined the socially unfit as: (1)the feeble-minded; (2)the pauper class; (3)the criminal class; (4)epileptics; (5)the insane; (6) the constitutionally weak, or the asthenic class; (7)those predisposed to specific diseases, or the diathetic class; (8) the deformed; (9) those having defective sense organs, the blind and deaf.

Their solution? Eliminate those deemed to be "*socially unfit.*" Their proposed solutions to achieve this goal included: Life segregation, Sterilization, Restrictive Marriage laws and Customs, Polygamy, Euthanasia, and Non-Malthusian Doctrine: the artificial interference to prevent conception.

To be clear, euthanasia means killing people.

To reiterate, this includes those suffering from disease and other medical conditions, including but not limited to, epilepsy, allergies, asthma, the blind and deaf, and of course, they also wanted to kill convicted criminals.

Since sodomy was illegal in every state until 1962, gay men could be targeted for killing.

This was also a period where states had enacted "*Jim Crow*" racial segregation laws. Interracial marriage was considered a felony in many states. Under eugenics theory, this means anyone found guilty of a violation of anti-segregation or interracial marriage laws should and could be put to death as well.

Eugenicists were calling for nothing less than multi-pronged genocide.

Ok, so now we know a bit about eugenics, how does this fit in with feminism?

Prominent feminist Margaret Sanger was also an outspoken proponent of eugenics. Margaret Sanger is known as the founder of Planned Parenthood and considered a prominent feminist icon. Many of Ms. Sanger's writings are publicly available through the Margaret Sanger project, which has a publicly searchable online archive of her writings and speeches. Her words stir a great deal of controversy and so she's been publicly accused of being a genocidal racist who attempted to use sterilization and birth control to exterminate African-Americans in the United States. While her supporters tirelessly attempt to defend her genocidal ideologies through a combination of deflections and denials, her own words prove the brutal reality of her bigotry.

As a result, many of the things she's advocated remain controversial, even today.

On December 29, 1912, as part of a series of articles published in the New York Call, a daily newspaper, Sanger wrote an article called Sexual Impulses: Part II. In it, she states,

> *"In all fish and reptiles where there is no great brain development, there is also no conscious sexual control. The lower down in the scale of human development we go the less sexual control we find.*
>
> *It is said that the aboriginal Australian, the lowest known species of the human family, just a step higher than the chimpanzee in brain development, has so little sexual control that police authority alone prevents*

> him from obtaining sexual satisfaction on the streets. According to one writer, the rapist has just enough brain development to raise him above the animal, but like the animal, when in heat knows no law except nature which impels him to procreate whatever the result."

In 1917, Sanger founded the Birth Control Review. While she openly advocated both abortion and birth control, she also used her magazine as a platform to advocate her white supremacist and genocidal eugenic views.

Sanger hated the poor. In December 1917, Sanger penned, "*Birth Control: Margaret Sanger's Reply to Theodore Roosevelt*" published in the Metropolitan Magazine, where she argues in favor of birth control as a means of limiting the population of the poor. In her article, she opines,

> "*There is no greater national waste than the spawning of the slums.*" It's important to know that many minorities and immigrants lived in slums in this time period.

In May 1919, she penned an editorial which she stated,

> "*The effort toward racial progress that is being made to-day by the medical profession, by social workers, by the various charitable and philanthropic organizations and by state institutions for the physically and mentally unfit is practically wasted. All these forces are in a very emphatic sense marking time. They will continue to mark time until the medical profession recognizes the fact that the ever-increasing tide of the unfit is overwhelming all these agencies are doing for society.*"

On March 25, 1925, at a pioneer dinner, while giving a speech, Sanger said,

> "*The United States Government has become a pioneer by its immigration laws. It is really putting into effect today in it immigration laws, exactly what most Birth Controllers want. The only thing is, while it applies its laws in keeping out of this country the mentally defective and the physically weak and defective, the paupers and the other kind of so-called undesirables, we only wish it would extend its laws a little bit more and stop the multiplication of the same undesirable type within.*"

In her March 3, 1938, speech, "*Human Conservation And Birth Control,*" Sanger openly supported Hitler's Nazi racial-purity forced-sterilization laws for women and openly advocated the United States enact laws patterned after Nazi Germany.

In an unpublished draft, undated, Sanger writes,

> *One authority claims that out of our population of one hundred million only fifteen million can be regarded as intelligent. That eighty-five million have less than average mental capacity and compare to the youth of fifteen years--under this comes the morons, feebleminded, high grade imbeciles, then idiots, etc. From this grade come paupers, prostitutes, criminals, tramps, inebriates, all tending to be born somewhat defective.*

In the same draft, Sanger goes on to state,

> "*This group are lacking in vitality, in moral*

> *standards, in initiative and are wholly unfit for organized activity. Bad conditions kill off the unfit, leaving room and space for the fit to survive. In allowing the unfit to reproduce their kind we are doing our best to lower the level of life."*

On December 10, 1939, Margaret Sanger wrote a letter to Dr. C.J. Gamble. Her letter was requesting that Dr. Gamble keep in touch with her about their *"Negro Project."* In her letter she states,

> *"There is only one thing that I would like to be in touch with and that is the Negro Project...*
>
> *Miss Rose sent me a copy of your letter of December 5th and I note that you doubt it worthwhile to employ a full time Negro physician. It seems to me from my experience where I have been in North Carolina, Georgia, Tennessee and Texas, that while the colored Negroes have great respect for white doctors they can get closer to their own members and more or less lay their cards on the table which means their ignorance, superstitions and doubts. They do not do this with the white people and if we can train the Negro doctor at the Clinic he can go among them with enthusiasm and with knowledge, which, I believe, will have far-reaching results among the colored people. His work in my opinion should be entirely with the Negro profession and the nurses, hospital, social workers, as well as the County's white doctors. His success will depend upon his personality and his training by us."*

Now, you might ask, what was the Negro Project's goal here? Well, later in the letter, she's very candid about that. She says,

> *"We do not want word to go out that we want to exterminate the Negro population"*

Sanger's goal was to use birth control and abortion to "exterminate" African-Americans. Like I said, she's genocidal racist.

Sanger, while a vocal advocate for Planned Parenthood and feminism, used her platform to further her secret eugenics agenda of genocidal extermination of everyone not of her race and elite social status.

Remember though, feminism means equality.

Now here's what surprises me the most: Black women openly embrace both feminism and Planned Parenthood's abortion advocacy.

Fun Fact: In 1910, Blacks made up about 15% of the American population, at the time of this writing, it's under to 13%. Put another way, in just over 100 years since Planned Parenthood started killing unborn African American children, the 2% nationwide population reduction represents close to a 12% decrease of the number of African Americans in the United States.

It's a tragedy that Planned Parenthood targets African-American communities for birth control and abortion. They've brain-washed black feminists to become lambs to lead to the slaughter.

Like most prominent feminists, Margaret Sanger's hypocrisy and hidden agendas are a hard act to follow. However, Gloria Steinem's feminist career takes it to the next level.

Gloria was born to Ruth and Leo Steinem in 1934. While the history books try to sugar coat it, Gloria's mom was mentally ill and prone to violence. According to the Jewish Woman's Archive, her father, during the winters, was a traveling antique dealer who often took his family with him on these excursions. In the summer, her father owned and operated a beach resort in Clarke Lake, Michigan.

The Jewish Women's Archive also reports that Gloria, as a little girl, *"apprenticed"* herself to nightclub entertainers. Gloria's parents divorced in 1945 when she was 11 years old. After the divorce, Gloria and her mom lived in Toledo, Ohio. When she was a young teen, Gloria *"performed"* in nightclubs for $10 a night. Later she got a job as a "salesgirl" after school and on weekends. Then when Gloria was 16, the Jewish Women's Archive reports,

> *"The following year, she was rescued by Susanne, who persuaded their father, despite the divorce, to take over Ruth's care for one year so that Gloria could get away and live with her sister in Washington, D.C."*

That begs the question: What did Gloria need rescuing from?

Upon closer examination, the answer might lie in the wage she earned as a young teen nightclub entertainer. Gloria earned $10 a night. In 1946, the minimum wage was 40 cents an hour. At 13 years old, assuming Gloria was working four hours a night, she was earning $2.50 an hour. Seems like a lot of money for a young unskilled teen girl to earn working in a nightclub in Toledo, Ohio, doesn't it?

With Gloria's mom being unable to work due to her

mental disability, was Gloria forced into child prostitution to keep them from being homeless? I know its scandalous. However, given the facts, it's a legitimate question.

We may never know the answer to this question. However, if this was the case and her older sister Susanne found out, it rationally explains how Susanne was able to successfully convince her father to return to Toledo to care for his mentally ill ex-wife.

Full disclosure, (I know this may come as a surprise) I'm not a Gloria Steinem fan. I haven't read any Gloria Steinem biographies. However, from my research of many other sources, I haven't been able to find any source that addresses this issue.

Gloria moved in with her older sister in Washington DC. According to Western High School's Arts Alumni Association, Gloria graduated from Western High, 47th out of 141 students. She was then accepted to Smith college and while attending college, according to the Jewish Women's Archives, she spent her Junior year in Geneva and a summer in Oxford.

1956 was a busy year for Gloria. She graduated from Smith College, had an abortion in London, and received a Chester Bowles Asian Fellowship that sent her to India, from 1956 to 1958. While in India, Gloria claims to have authored and published a government-sponsored guidebook entitled, *"The 1000 Indias."*

When Steinem returned to the United States in 1958, she was recruited by the CIA to create and direct the CIA funded *"Independent Research Service."* To reiterate, this organization was entirely funded by and dependent on the CIA. It was a CIA front.

As an undercover CIA agent, Steinem recruited over 100 members for the Independent Research Service. At the direction of the CIA, they attended the World Youth Festival in 1959 in Vienna and the next one held in 1962 in Helsinki.

None of Steinem's CIA associations were made public until 1967 when Ramparts magazine published an article exposing her CIA connections. Once her involvement was known, Steinem confirmed the story in interviews with the Washington Post, the New York Times, and a TV interview. However, in each of these interviews, she reframed her involvement as merely receiving funding from the CIA and claimed they wanted nothing in return.

Naively and amazingly, everyone thought her story was totally legit. This is probably because of the CIA's well-documented history of providing random women extremely large cash grants to attend European festivals.

Who knew?

However, in the 1970s, more facts about Steinem's CIA employment appeared that directly contradicted the narrative she initially painted in her 1967 interviews. Yet, the criticism didn't come from enemies from the misogynistic mythical patriarchy, but from within the feminist movement itself.

Redstockings, one of the first second-wave radical feminist organizations formed in the United States, issued a damning press release about Steinem. It directly questioned the credibility of Steinem's CIA involvement and her identity as a strong independent woman who got rich from her own hard work.

Their press release was published, in a slightly edited

form, in the July 1975 edition of the feminist magazine, "*Off Our Backs.*" Interestingly, before publishing the press release, Off Our Backs editorial staff withheld it an extra month to conduct more research to make sure they did their due diligence to make sure they were publishing verifiable facts and reasonably credible allegations based on those facts. After completing this additional review of Redstockings investigation, Off Our Backs editorial staff made the following statements about their investigation of Steinem,

> "*We all feel that the Redstockings should be praised for three things. They have undertaken a much needed analysis of Ms. magazine which no other radical group has attempted...the Redstockings spent an entire year on this project, which enabled them to do considerable in-depth reporting. Finally, we admire the Redstockings for having the courage to make themselves vulnerable by calling Steinem personally to account.*"

Clearly, even in the 1970s, Steinem was an extremely powerful force to contend with. Yet, feminists claim that this was a time when women were treated as second-class citizens.

What exactly was Redstockings issue with Steinem and her 1967 portrayal of the CIA created Independent Research Service?

Redstockings raised concerns over Steinem's CIA sponsored attendance at the World Youth Festivals. They discovered Steinem's organization was creating detailed dossiers on many of the festival's attendants. At both festivals, they reported that Steinem's Independent Research Service very vocally criticized planned festival activities. At the 1962 festival, rioting broke out for four nights targeting the festival itself and 40 people ended up arrested. *Pravda*, a Russian newspaper, blamed the riots on the CIA.

Redstockings claims these prove Steinem was not merely receiving free money from the CIA but that she was also a government sponsored agitator. Steinem practically admits this claim in her 1967 news interviews.

Also, Redstockings takes issue with Steinem's claim she left the Independent Research Service in 1962. They discovered Steinem remained a member of the Independent Research Service's board of directors of until at least 1969 when *"Who's Who in America,"* in their 1968-1969 edition, had Steinem listed as:

> *"Director, educational foundation, Independent Research Service, Cambridge, Mass, N.Y.C, 1959-1962, now member Board of Directors, Washington."*

Off Our Backs discovered that before Who's Who publishes information on a person, they reach out to that person and give them a data sheet to allow the person to send their own information.

When confronted, Steinem claimed Who's Who made a mistake. At the time of this writing, Who's Who has never issued a retraction or a correction for Steinem's original entry.

When Redstockings started investigating Steinem, apparently, they completely hated her. They tried to fact check her entire life. Consequently, they investigated her time in India from 1956-1958. They discovered the Chester Bowles Asian Fellowship that funded Steinem's two years in India, including round-trip airfare, didn't exist. That's right. Steinem was the only person in the history of the world who is documented as receiving it. No one has received it before or after her.

This author has attempted to verify the existence of a Chester Bowles Fellowship without success. However, what I did find was the existence of a man named Chester Bowles. Believe it or not, Chester Bowles isn't a very common name.

President Truman appointed Chester as the U.S. Ambassador to both India and Nepal from 1951 to 1953. Chester later served as a U.S. Congressman and afterward, was reappointed as a U.S. Ambassador. Because diplomatic agents were often considered spies, combined with the fact no one can verify the existence of a Fellowship named after Chester, Redstockings believed the Chester Bowles Asian Fellowship was a cover for CIA funding. Based on the verifiable facts surrounding Steinem, this author believes Redstockings exercised sound reasoning and their conclusion appears logical.

It makes you wonder what was the nature of Steinem's relationship to Chester Bowles.

Further, Redstockings attempted to verify the Steinem authored travel guide, "*A 1000 Indias.*" Turns out, this claim was also specious. Not only could Redstockings not find any source to verify Steinem authored this book, they couldn't find any evidence of any book by that name ever being published anywhere. Further, When Off Our Backs editorial staff fact-checked Redstockings investigation, they discovered an article from the Chicago Tribune where Steinem stated her book on India was published by Air India. The editorial staff contacted Air India and the Indian Embassy and no one had ever heard of the book.

This author also attempted to verify the existence of Steinem's book, *"A 1000 Indias"* without success.

Then...and perhaps most damning...Redstockings attacked Steinem's very identity as a strong independent and self-made female entrepreneur.

Enter Clay Felker.

Clay graduated from Duke University in 1951 and according to the Guardian's July 28, 2008, obituary, he was the "features" editor of Esquire in 1957 and according to the Washington Post's obituary, he left in late 1962.

Redstockings discovered Felker attended the 1962 summer World Youth Festival in Helsinki as part of the CIA front organization directed by Steinem, Independent Research Service. Clay was the editor of the CIA financed Independent Research Service's newspaper that was published daily during the festival. When confronted, Clay denied CIA involvement. However, I find it highly unlikely, as editor of a CIA-financed newspaper, he would've been that ignorant. In fact, he practically admits he knew the CIA was backing him when he told reporters he went to oppose communists.

Why is this footnote in history important?

The Helsinki festival was held during the summer 1962. Almost immediately after returning from their CIA trip, Steinem persuaded Felker to hire her as a freelance writer to pen an article for Esquire. He was still its editor. The original article Steinem wrote was so bad she admitted he forced her to rewrite it. Steinem's article, "The Moral Disarmament of Betty Coed" was not only featured in the September 1962 issue of Esquire, Felker had it labeled as the Editor's Pick. Yet, this was Steinem's debut article.

It's highly unusual for an unknown author, who's writing was so bad her work needed to be entirely rewritten, to receive such high praise for a debut article in Esquire. To clarify, Felker not only provided Steinem a platform for her writing, but he gave her the strongest editorial endorsement he could give any author. Whatever happened in Helsinki, it's clear Steinem had Felker under a spell. Felker, from this point forward, was Steinem's sugar daddy and white knight.

Within three months of publishing Steinem's article, Felker left Esquire.

Steinem returned to her teen nightclub entertainment roots and landed a job at the New York Playboy Club becoming a bunny. She later wrote about her job, reframing it as, "undercover journalism." While her freelance article about was picked up by Show magazine, it tanked her journalism career. She became largely unemployable, because, in her words: "I had now become a Bunny..."

In 1968, Felker rescued Steinem by hiring her to work at his newly founded New York magazine. This time, however, Felker hired her as a full-time employee instead of a mere freelance writer. Felker gave Steinem her own column.

In 1972, Steinem and Felker created Ms. magazine. The first issue of Ms. Magazine was an approximately 40-page special-edition insert included in Felker's highly successful New York magazine. Thus, Steinem was able to take advantage New York magazine's established success, reputation, and its large distribution network.

While Felker's involvement was publicly muted, Ms. Magazine would've never been published had Felker not completely funded it. He allowed Steinem access to his vast network of distribution, publishing, and advertising resources. While it's not stated anywhere, it seems obvious Felker not only fully funded the project, he oversaw it from beginning to end.

Felker's inclusion of Ms. in the New York magazine led to Steinem's Ms. magazine to receive 26,000 subscription orders. Oddly, it appears Felker, even though he provided 100% of the investment, took no ownership interest. This is highly unusual since a large amount of initial subscription sales from the first issue foreshadowed huge profitability.

Another oddity about Ms. magazine is that after Felker published the first issue, Warner Communications stepped and financed the magazine. New York Times reporter Geraldine Fabrikant reported on May 9, 1987, that Warner Communications financed the entire magazine, investing $1 million dollars. However, other sources revealed that even though Warner provided all the financing, it only took a 25% ownership interest.

Warner Communications actions make no business sense.

It makes you wonder, what inspired Felker to white knight Steinem's entire career? He's responsible for almost completely funding and establishing Steinem's success on the national stage. If it weren't for Felker, Steinem wouldn't have the influence she has today.

When Redstockings discovered these facts, they rightly became concerned. It appeared that every milestone Steinem claimed to achieve independently, was either unverifiable or discovered to be funded by others, including the CIA and sugar daddy Clay Felker.

The next time a guy feels badly because he allowed a woman to take advantage of him, tell him the story of Clay Felker's white knighting of Gloria Steinem. Beyond possibly sleeping together, I don't think Felker got anything else out of their relationship.

What happened after Redstockings disclosed the findings of their investigation?

Village Voice reporter Nancy Borman, on May 21, 1979, published the entire story in her article, "*Inside the CIA with Gloria Steinem.*"

She reports that the Redstockings self-published a book entitled, "*Feminist Revolution*" that included an entire chapter on the Steinem/CIA connection. It printed and sold all 5000 copies. In order to print more books, Redstockings approached Random House to publish more copies. After Random House's legal team vetted their book, Random house agreed to print 20,000 copies of the "*Feminist Revolution*" and scheduled it to hit the stores in June 1976.

Shortly afterwards, Gloria Steinem herself went to Random House and hand-delivered a letter from her attorney threatening to sue unless the CIA chapter was removed from the book. A few weeks later, Sugar Daddy Clay Felker, the Women's Action Alliance, Warner Communications, Franklin Thomas, The Overseas Education Fund of the League of Women Voters, and Katherine Graham all threatened to sue Random House. Interesting, everyone one of those threatening to sue were either financially invested in Steinem or had CIA connections

As a result, the book publishing was delayed almost

three years and despite having 13,000 advanced orders...Random House would only publish 12,500 copies. Once it hit the shelves, the chapter on Steinem's CIA connections had been deleted entirely.

Redstockings lost their mind. After the censored version of the book was published, they held a press conference decrying Random House's censorship. They were so incensed at the press conference, they provided an 18-page answer to Random House's objections to the publication of the Steinem material. When the credibility of Redstockings' investigation was challenged, they produced detailed documentation to back up their claims. Borman states there was a near total media blackout of the Steinem/Random House censorship controversy.

At the time of this writing, the Village Voice has posted archives of its past editions online. However, the May 1979 issue that included Borman's article is curiously absent. I was only able to find it online by virtue of locating a message board discussing the book, *"Blacklisted News, Secret History from Chicago '69 to 1984"* which published Borman's entire article there.

Clearly, the near total media blackout on Steinem's CIA connections that Borman lamented about in 1979 continues today.

Knowing Steinem's entire career and identity is built on lies financed by others, is it any wonder that Steinem's National Organization of Women gave Emma Sulkowicz, a confirmed false rape accuser and a liar, an award for courage?

Oh, in case you didn't know, Steinem co-founded the National Organization of Women. Guess liars like to stick together.

When feminists try to paint their history as one of strong independent heroines overcoming the mythical patriarchy, remind them that Sanger's and Steinem's success was only possible on the shoulders of wealthy corporate sugar daddies and white knights. Simply put, they were only successful because of corporate welfare.

More importantly, if you look at almost every modern rich feminist, they follow the same template: get some rich sugar-daddy or organization to bankroll them with the corporate welfare necessary to subsidize their success, then claim they did it themselves while denying the existence of the welfare they received.

3 PATRIARCHY AND MALE PRIVILEGE

Before we discuss patriarchy, we should probably first define it. Looking again to Merriam-Webster, patriarchy is defined, in pertinent part, as:

> *"social organization marked by the supremacy of the father in the clan or family, the legal dependence of wives and children, and the reckoning of descent and inheritance in the male line"*

The United States and the Western world used to technically be governed by patriarchal policies. However, this was more of a limited or soft patriarchy that was founded in culture norms of the time. It wasn't one inspired out of any expressed wish to control or oppress women. In fact, there's plenty of evidence in history - with the notable exception of Islam - that no large or well-established governments were ever implemented for the expressed purpose of oppressing women.

U.S. President John F. Kennedy signed the equal pay act in 1963, ending the last of the soft patriarchal government policies. The act requited working women to be paid the same as male counterparts performing the same job, with the same level of experience. Forty-three years prior, American women won the right to vote.

In 1880, women had a "woman only" stock exchange, founded by Mary Gage. The first "woman only" bank, The First Woman's Bank of Tennessee, was opened in 1919 in Clarkesville, Tennessee. Although, all the shareholders were men, it was managed and directed exclusively by women.

Clearly, the shareholders didn't get the "oppress women" memo.

One of the main targets of the feminists since the movement gained prominence has been its war on marriage and family values. Linda Gordon, feminist author and professor even went so far as to state,

> *"The nuclear family must be destroyed...whatever its ultimate meaning, the break-up of families now is an objectively revolutionary process...no woman should have to deny herself of any opportunities because of her special responsibility to her children..."*

Vivian Gornick, another feminist author stated,

> *"being a housewife is an illegitimate profession."*

Sheila Cronin, the leader of the National Organization of

Women stated,

> "*Since marriage constitutes slavery for women, it is clear that the women's movement must concentrate on attacking this institution.*"

These are just a few of many statements made by prominent feminist leaders and voices within the movement in opposition to marriage and family values.

Why is this important?

Well, decades later, it appears feminism has, in large part, achieved its goal of the destruction of marriage and family values.

According to the CDC/NCHS National Vital Statistics System, as of 2014, the rate of marriage per 1000 people in the United States is about 6.9 and the rate of divorce is 3.2. These numbers are based on the 2010 census. This means that, as of 2014, the annual divorce rate is just over 46%. More striking is that the divorce rate goes up with each successive marriage, about 60% for a second marriage and about 73% for a third marriage.

On August 22, 2015, Science Daily published an article that discussed a study conducted by Michael Rosenfeld, associate professor of sociology at Stanford University, entitled, "*How Couples meet and Stay Together.*" In this study, Rosenfeld found that when married couples divorce, 69% of the time, the divorce was initiated by the wife.

However, the feminist victory over the institution of marriage and family values came with a steep price tag.

The community cost of divorce and broken homes has been known for over 20 years. On March 17, 1995, the

Heritage Foundation published a report entitled, "*The Real Root Causes of Violent Crime: The Breakdown of Marriage, Family, and Community,*" authored by Patrick F. Fagan, Ph.D.

Here's the key finding of Fagan's report,

> "*The scholarly evidence...suggests that at the heart of the explosion of crime in America is the loss of the capacity of fathers and mothers to be responsible in caring for the children they bring into the world. This loss of love and guidance at the intimate levels of marriage and family has broad social consequences...for the wider community.*"

As you can see, Dr. Fagan's key finding demonstrates the societal consequences of feminism's war on marriage and family values.

The report's findings break down these social consequences very concisely as follows,

> "*Over the past thirty years, the rise in violent crime parallels the rise in families abandoned by fathers.*
>
> *High-crime neighborhoods are characterized by high concentrations of families abandoned by fathers.*
>
> *State-by-state analysis by Heritage scholars indicates that a 10 percent increase in the percentage of children living in single-parent homes leads typically to a 17 percent increase in juvenile crime.*
>
> *The rate of violent teenage crime*

> *corresponds with the number of families abandoned by fathers.*
>
> *The type of aggression and hostility demonstrated by a future criminal often is foreshadowed in unusual aggressiveness as early as age five or six.*
>
> *The future criminal tends to be an individual rejected by other children as early as the first grade who goes on to form his own group of friends, often the future delinquent gang."*

Not only did the report look at the societal impacts of absent fathers, it also looked at homes where the biological family remained intact. To this end, the report contrasts neighborhoods of families of children where the marriage remains intact and family values are practiced.

> *"Neighborhoods with a high degree of religious practice are not high-crime neighborhoods.*
>
> *Even in high-crime inner-city neighborhoods, well over 90 percent of children from safe, stable homes do not become delinquents. By contrast only 10 percent of children from unsafe, unstable homes in these neighborhoods avoid crime.*
>
> *Criminals capable of sustaining marriage gradually move away from a life of crime after they get married.*
>
> *The mother's strong affectionate attachment to her child is the child's best buffer against a life of crime.*

> *The father's authority and involvement in raising his children are also a great buffer against a life of crime."*

The differences between communities that embrace the feminist view that marriage should be destroyed, when compared to the communities where marriage and traditional family values remained intact are striking. They show that the single largest contributing factor to high levels of neighborhood crime is fatherless families. Put another way, broken families, where the biological mother and biological father have separated, are directly responsible for the increase in the crime rate of their communities.

This makes it brutally clear that the feminist perspective on families and marriage is harmful to children and communities because feminism's war on marriage is directly responsible for creating families without fathers.

Almost 20 years later, Robert I. Lerman and W. Bradford Wilcox of the American Enterprise Institute for Family Studies confirm Dr. Fagan's 1995 findings and their work demonstrates that intact families are necessary for economic prosperity in communities. In October 2014, they coauthored a 56-page report, *"For Richer, For Poorer, How Family Structures Economic Success in America."* This report made five key findings,

> *1. The retreat from marriage – a retreat that has been concentrated among lower-income Americans – plays a key role in the changing economic fortunes of American family life. We estimate that the growth in median income of families with children would be 44 percent higher if the United States enjoyed 1980 levels of married parenthood today. Further, at least 32*

percent of the growth in family-income inequality since 1979 among families with children and 37 percent of the decline in men's employment rates during that time can be linked to the decreasing number of Americans who form and maintain stable, married families.

2. Growing up with both parents (in an intact family) is strongly associated with more education, work, and income among today's young men and women. Young men and women from intact families enjoy an annual "intact-family premium" that amounts to $6,500 and $4,700, respectively, over the incomes of their peers from single-parent families.

3. Men obtain a substantial "marriage premium" and women bear no marriage penalty in their individual incomes, and both men and women enjoy substantially higher family incomes, compared to peers with otherwise similar characteristics. For instance, men enjoy a marriage premium of at least $15,900 per year in their individual income compared to their single peers.

4. These two trends reinforce each other. Growing up with both parents increases your odds of becoming highly educated, which in turn leads to higher odds of being married as an adult. Both the added education and marriage result in higher income levels. Indeed, men and women who were raised with both parents present and then go on to marry enjoy an especially high income as adults. Men and women who are currently married and were raised in an *intact family enjoy an annual "family premium" in their household income that exceeds that of their unmarried peers who were raised in nonintact families by at least $42,000.*

5. The advantages of growing up in an intact family and being married extend across the population. They apply about as much to blacks and Hispanics as they do to whites. For instance, black men enjoy a marriage premium of at least $12,500 in their individual income compared to their single peers. The advantages also apply, for the most part, to men and women who are less educated. For instance, men with a high-school degree or less enjoy a marriage premium of at least $17,000 compared to their single peers.

By destroying institution of marriage and the family values associated with it, feminists are destroying our communities. In real terms, Milo Yiannopoulos was right when he said,

"feminism is cancer."

The next main target of feminist ire belongs to their belief that all men benefit from "male privilege." Interestingly, the term male privilege, at the time of this writing, doesn't exist in any established dictionary. However, the Urban Dictionary has multiple definitions of the term. Amusingly, the top definition is,

"A fictional term made by butt hurt lesbians, with hair shorter than their intelligence, to use as an excuse for anything and everything."

> *Example: "I went to court for stabbing a man, because he said I looked like a pig, and then I was arrested because male privilege."*

The second most popular definition from the Urban Dictionary is,

> *"A myth fabricated and spread by feminists, primarily liberal and progressive ones, to use as the excuse for why women are not dominating every aspect of life including politics, STEM, and other jobs. This conspiracy theory automatically assumes all men are not only successful as a whole, but that they have only earned what they have because of their gender. To believe in the existence of male privilege one must also believe that the world is controlled by the patriarchy."*

Even though feminists use the myth of "male privilege" as their excuse for why men are more successful than them, even Urban Dictionary doesn't give it any credibility.

With that in mind, a major issue with feminist ideology is that it advocates for rights and privileges on behalf of women. Yet, feminists oppose any policy that places equitable responsibility on women in return for these rights. Finally let's look at the U.S. military draft. For adult men, if they refuse to register for the draft, they're barred from voting and from receiving any kind of grants or loans to attend college. At the time of this writing, women don't have to register for the U.S. military draft, but are allowed to both vote and receive financial grants and loans for college.

Further, if feminists are so concerned about the gender

gaps in Western society, why are they ignoring the epidemic of homeless men?

In July 2001, Healing Hands, a magazine put out by the National Health Care for the Homeless Council (NHCHC), reported,

> *"Men compromise 77% of single homeless adults...approximately 33% of them are military veterans...homeless men are more than twice as likely to have an alcohol or drug addiction. Of homeless clients reporting alcohol, drug or mental health problems, 73% are male. Homeless men are...more frequently excluded from emergency shelters...Single Homeless men are at increased risk for chronic homelessness."*

Healing Hands interviewed professionals who work with the homeless to get an idea of how often people become homeless out of choice. They interviewed Jeff Singer, MSW, and President and CEO of Health Care for the Homeless Inc in Baltimore Maryland. At the time of the interview, Singer had worked with over 10,000 homeless and stated that he has,

> *"never met anyone who said that he prefers to live on the street, be cold and dirty, and have difficulty finding food and shelter."*

When Healing Hands interviewed Eddie Bonin, FNP, who provides healthcare for homeless youth, typically ages, 18-24, they write,

> *"Most of his clients are male. A history of child abuse is an impetus for many of these youth to leave home, he says. Once they are living on the street, they often get involved*

> *in "survival sex" with either gender,*
> *regardless of sexual orientation, just to get*
> *money, food and a place to stay."*

Mona Chalabi reported in the Guardian on May 7, 2013,

> *"The housing charity Crisis found that 84%*
> *of the hidden homeless were male. And the*
> *latest CHAIN figures suggest that 9 out of*
> *10 sleeping rough are male.*
>
> *According to Mankind Initiative, in UK*
> *refuges or safe houses, there are 33 spaces*
> *dedicated to male victims of domestic*
> *violence (of which 18 are for gay males*
> *only), compared to around 4,000 spaces*
> *reserved for females."*

Interestingly, while feminists loudly proclaim from the highest parapet that their goal is to end gender inequality, when it comes to male homelessness, their silence is deafening. It's clear their silence is just another demonstration that their goal isn't gender equality, but rather gynocentric superiority.

The next area of complaint feminism often levels is that women aren't equitably represented in the job market. On the surface, this may seem a legitimate complaint. However, once again, the facts tell a far different story.

On September 6, 2016, NPR interviewed Nicholas Eberstadt, an economic and demographic researcher at American Enterprise Institute and author of *"Men Without Work."* He stated,

> *"One in six prime-age guys has no job; it's*
> *kind of worse than it was in the depression*
> *in 1940."*

On June 20, 2016, The Washington Post published an article entitled, *"Why America's men aren't working."* At the time of the article, the national unemployment rate was 4.7%. However, while the unemployment rate was very low, the Washington Post states,

> *"There's one statistic that has been vexing economists. The size of the nation's workforce, known as the labor force participation rate, continues to fall. Since the downtown, the percentage of that population that has a job or is looking for one has dropped...to 62.6%, a level not seen since the 1970s."*

Think about that for a minute. That means that the 62.6% number isn't the number of people working. It's the number of people working in addition to those looking for work. The number of people who are actually working is lower.

Does this constitute evidence that women aren't able to look for work? No. The Washington Post goes on to state,

> *"The White House's Council of Economic Advisers...found that the United States has the third lowest participation rate for "prime-age men" among the worlds' developed countries.*
>
> *"The CEA's analysis looks at several common theories behind why so many American men have dropped out of the job market. Legions of women have joined the workforce....women's participation rate topped 50% in the late 1970s and peaked at about 60% in the early 2000s."*

Pew Research, in January 2017, published a graph that shows men's participation rate in the workforce has declined by 15% since 1999. Women's participation rate has increased by 22% during that same time.

Yet, based on workforce participation rate, it doesn't seem like women are very under-represented at all.

How to the genders compare when it comes to higher education?

According to the National Girls Collaborative Project, in 2013, women earned 57% of all bachelor's degrees in science and engineering. They also earned 50.3% of all bachelor's degrees. Science Alert, on June 24, 2016, reported that Dartmouth college had reported,

> *"it had more women than men graduate from its engineering course this year"*

The National Center for Education Statistics is the primary federal entity for collecting and analyzing data related to education in the United States. They're located within the U.S. Department of Education and the Institute of Education Sciences under U.S. Congressional mandate. For 2016, they report,

> *"Females are expected to account for the majority of college students: about 11.7 million females will attend in fall 2016, compared with 8.8 million males."*

Let that sink in.

In 2016, 2.9 million more women than men were anticipated to be enrolled in U.S. colleges. That's about 33% more women attending college than men.

Yet, to hear feminists tell it, the mythical patriarchy and

male privilege have discriminated against women and prevented them from obtaining a higher education. Again, the facts show that this is just another feminist myth.

Now that we have an idea of where gender inequality actually exists, in what areas of society are men over-represented, other than homelessness?

Well, men are far more likely to be killed on the job than women. In June 1996, Andrew Knestaut reported in the Census of Fatal Occupational Injuries,

> "*Of the nation's employed workers, 46% are women, yet they accounted for just 8% of the nation's job related fatalities.*"

Then we fast-forward almost 20 years and the American Enterprise Institute, on April 9, 2013, reports this hasn't really changed at all,

> "*As in previous years, the chart above shows the significant gender disparity in workplace fatalities: 4,234 men died on the job (92% of the total) in 2011 compared to only 375 women (8% of the total). The "gender occupational fatality gap" in 2011 was considerable — more than 11 men died on the job for every woman who died while working.*"

Feminism clearly hasn't closed the occupational fatality gap. As long as men remain the majority of the casualties, feminists don't care. This is just another example of how feminist ideology practices situational ethics. Rather than try to cut the male workplace fatality rate, they ignore it. It's gynocentrism at the cost of men's lives.

Nowhere can the man-hating consequences of feminism's war on men, marriage, and family values be seen more starkly than in the arena of suicide.

It's been common knowledge for decades that men commit suicide at far higher rates than women.

Why are men more likely to commit suicide than women?

Dr. Susan J. Blumenthal served for more than two decades as a top federal government health official in four U.S. Presidential administrations. In her paper, *"Suicide and Gender,"* on her website, Dr. Blumenthal states that being recently separated and divorced are risk factors associated with suicide. She states,

> *"Suicide is more common among those who are...recently separated, divorced...The suicide rates are second highest for divorced men."*

On September 24, 2012, Alice G. Walton penned *"The Gender Inequality of Suicide: Why Are Men At Such High Risk?"* for Forbes Magazine. In her article, she discusses a new 155-page research report published and released by Samaritans in September 2012. Samaritans is a suicide prevention organization founded in 1953. They're one of the largest organizations of their kind in the world and not only do they help those considering suicide through real-time advocacy. They also conduct research into suicide prevention.

While the Forbes article is interesting, it's clear it ignores the focus on the Samaritan study in favor of overly ambiguous language and weasel words and attempts to reframe her writing as a woman's issue. I know this is a strong criticism, but I think after looking at her article when compared with the report itself, you might better understand my criticism.

She can't even go an entire paragraph with trying to change the focus to women. She writes,

> *"In just about every country, men commit suicide more frequently than women, which is intriguing since women typically have higher (at least, reported) rates of mental health disorders like depression."*

This statement sets the tone for the rest of the article, which degenerates into intellectual dishonesty. Again, I know this is harsh, so you'd rightly ask: why the harsh criticism?

Well, let's look at the research report itself. Right at the beginning of the research report, the executive summary, quoted in its entirety, debunks Alice's entire premise,

> *"This report seeks to explain why men of low socio-economic position in their mid-years are excessively vulnerable to death by suicide and provides recommendations to reduce these unnecessary deaths.*
>
> *The report goes beyond the existing body of suicide research and the statistics, to try and understand life for this group of men, and why they may come to feel without purpose, meaning or value.*
>
> *The key message from the report is that suicide needs to be addressed as a health and gender inequality – an avoidable difference in health and length of life that results from being poor and disadvantaged; and an issue*

> *that affects men more because of the way society expects them to behave. It is time to extend suicide prevention beyond its focus on individual mental health problems, to understand the social and cultural context which contributes to people feeling they wish to die."*

Yet, Alice tries to reframe male suicide as a mental health issue...because...reasons. This was the exact opposite of the findings of Samaritans' research. They found gender inequality against men as the major contributing factor.

To bring this into even more perspective, the report cites,

> *"Relationship breakdown is more likely to lead men, rather than women, to suicide. Men rely more on their partners for emotional support and suffer this loss more acutely. Honour is also part of masculinity, and to be 'disrespected' in front of others by the actions of their partner (infidelity or abandonment) may lead to shame and/or impulsive reactions, perhaps to punish ex-partners. Men are more likely to be separated from their children and this plays a role in some men's suicides."*

This report is damning. It clearly demonstrates and links feminism's openly declared war on marriage and family values as a major cause that directly leads to men killing themselves.

In fact, you can tell my conclusions are directly supported by Samaritans because in order to effectively address this problem, they state,

> *"Samaritans calls on national government, statutory services (such as health, welfare, employment and social services), local authorities and the third sector to take action to reduce suicide in disadvantaged men in mid-life."*

In addition to calling on the government, at all levels, to address the gender inequality issue of male suicide they recommended, among other things, the following,

> *"Ensure that suicide prevention strategies include explicit aims to reduce socio-economic inequalities and gender inequalities in suicide.*
>
> *Enable inter-agency working to address the multiple difficulties experienced by men in mid-life...*
>
> *Provide therapies which address the specific psychological factors associated with suicide – particularly, for men...*
>
> *Develop innovative approaches to working with men that build on the ways men do 'get through' in everyday life."*

Why has this issue gotten so little media attention? This is groundbreaking work into one of the leading causes of death for men. It's because it conclusively and verifiably demonstrates that feminism's war on marriage is killing men.

Feminists are so terrified that their complicity in male suicide will be discovered they're going to great lengths to cover it up.

On April 24, 2014, Janet Bloomfield (aka *Judgybitch*)

penned an article entitled: "*Ex-Wife Drives her Husband to Commit Suicide and Now Claims His Note is Her Intellectual Property. You've Got to Be Kidding Me.*"

To summarize her blog post, a man, who committed suicide, according to his own suicide letter, he did so because he was persecuted during his divorce by a gender-biased family court system and the divorce process itself. Even more horrifying, when his ex found out about his suicide letter, she and her feminist attorneys sought to copyright the suicide note to prevent others from finding out how badly the feminist war on marriage has devastated men's lives.

Here's the suicide note, in its entirety, written by Christopher Mackney, obtained from an online link through an article published by A Voice For Men in April 2014,

> *"I never wanted to speak out about any of this. All I wanted was a fair and reasonable child support, fair and reasonable visitation with my children and be free to move on with my life. The only reason I chose to write a blog and speak out about the abuse was because I thought it would give me some kind of leverage, as I had none.*
>
> *I made it clear to my ex-wife's attorney that the family court was not allowing me to change the orders, I had no information about my children and my child support was far beyond my ability to pay.*
>
> *I was hoping for some act of good faith to let me know that they wanted to reduce the conflict. It never came, not in 5 years. I felt that my only recourse was to speak out about the abuse and injustice in order to get*

the legal and psychological help I needed to manage the conflict, so that we could both parent our children. I reached out to my ex-wife's attorney again to ask for ANY other alternative.

They offered none, so I started the blog. Even after I started my Blog, I reached out again to tell them I would take down the blog if a Guardian Ad Litem could be appointed for my children. They never responded. Dina knew this would be the outcome and didn't care. As long as I was gone and out of the children's lives.

In hindsight, I recognize that my reactions to being bullied, abused and denied access to my children gave my ex-wife's attorney the ammunition they were looking for to bring me into Court, but nothing I said or done would have made a difference. I was powerless. I thought that at some point a third party would be involved that would recognize that my reactions were from the emotional abuse; being denied access to my children and bullied in Court. The Court refused at least six requests for third party intervention. All of the research said that a third party was the recommended course of action in these situations. A third party was the only way to truly understand the conflict.

I was not the person being portrayed in family court. I had no control over anything. The Court would only listen to my ex-wife's attorney granting all of their motions and agreeing to all their "over reaching" remedies.

When I read online about the patterns of behavior of high conflict divorce and how my ex-wife was the one blocking access to the children and negatively interpreting everything I did, I spoke out and tried to address the source of conflict. No one would tell me I was wrong, but no one would speak out about the abuse on my behalf, not the Doctors or attorneys. Experts in psychology have called it abuse, but none would make such a 'diagnosis', which I could then take to Court to obtain relief. As long as the pattern of behavior was not called 'abuse', my reactions would not be viewed in its proper context by the Court.

The way I looked at it was that if I remained silent, the abuse would continue. It did. When I finally decided to speak out, they didn't care.

They didn't care about how it would affect Dr. Samenow, Judge Bellows, our children, themselves or anyone else. They were not going to take their foot off the back of my neck.

They were fully invested in having me out of my children's lives, permanently. Bullying and parental alienation are all forms of emotional abuse. Psychopathy is an emotional dysfunction. People with psychopathy are identified by how they handle conflict. It is the disturbing lack of empathy, guilt shame, remorse that give them away. They are completely unaffected by the distress of others. As long as they get what they want, you may never see that side of them.

If you are in a position of power or status, you will probably not see that side of them either. However, people that are close to them or are of little value to them, will eventually see the pattern. They will slowly begin to realize they are being controlled manipulated and 'gas lighted'. Without even realizing it, you learn to go along to get along. If you break from this, you will experience their wrath. I remember on Memorial Day 2008, when I went to pick up my children for lunch at their grandparents house, Pete Scamardo came outside to confront me. I looked at him and said "Pete, you are nothing but a bully.

He responded "That's right, and I love it!

He said this in front of Dina, he wife and my children. When I got in the car to take my children to lunch, my son asked me "Dad, what's a bully?

Pete Scamardo and Dina Mackney are the most 'successful' father/daughter psychopaths ever to fool the Court. Pete Scamardo has over 100 lawsuits in Fairfax County alone. The litigants in these cases can confirm the patterns. The entire Scamardo family was accused of fraud by Maryland National Bank for $80 Million. Pete and Dina also circumvented the Thoroughbred Ownership licensing laws of Virginia, Maryland and West Virginia. One of her friends from college now refers to her the 'c' word after seeing the real Dina, after working with her.

Most of you will not see that side of her,

unless you run into conflict. While I am the one that took my own life, this was a murder conceived and financed by Pete Scamardo who hired Jim Cottrell and Kyle Bartol the day after I discovered he was a murderer, and then paid over $1 Million in legal fees to make it happen.

People 'targeted' by psychopaths call it 'murder by suicide'. I was a good father to my children when I was in their lives. No one can dispute or deny that.

Dr. Samenow even admitted under oath that I had a 'palpable' relationship with my kids. I know I was an extremely loving and positive influence on their lives and it kills me that I even feel like I have to defend my parenting. My children were the only source of joy and happiness in my marriage.

For the Judge Bellows to deny parents and children a 'palpable relationship' and each other's love is corruption.

He did not want it to be known that Dr. Samenow committed fraud or that Judge Terrence Ney had a 'close relationship' with a convicted murderer or a parental alienator. The love that my daughter and I shared was truly special. She is a such a sweet, kind and gentle spirit. I am so sorry that I will not be there to see her grow into a beautiful woman. It absolutely crushed me to not be in her life over the last three years. I worked very hard as a father to build her confidence and self-esteem. She is smart, funny and considerate, but she didn't know it yet.

I pray that she realizes her strengths and her confidence in herself will continue to grow. I love you dearly, Lily. My son Jack was just entering Kindergarten, when I lost access to him. He is gregarious, outgoing and a great athlete. He is smart and fearless. He could have just as much fun by himself as he could with other kids. Even the older boys in our neighborhood wanted to play with Jack. It absolutely breaks my heart that I will not be able to help him grow into a man. I love you to, Jack. I miss you both so much. My identity was taken from me, as result of this process of family court.

When it began, I was a commercial real estate broker with CB Richard Ellis. I lived by the Golden rule and made a living by bringing parties together and finding the common ground. My reputation as a broker was built on my honesty and integrity. When it ended, I was broke, homeless, unemployed and had no visitation with my own children. I had no confidence and was paralyzed with fear that I would be going to jail whenever my ex-wife wanted. Nothing I could say or do would stop it. This is what being to death or 'targeted' by a psychopath looks like. This is the outcome.

I didn't somehow change into a 'high conflict' person or lose my ability to steer clear of the law.

I've had never been arrested, depressed, homeless or suicidal before this family court process. The stress and pressure applied to me was deliberate and nothing I could do or say would get me any relief. Nothing I or my attorneys said to my ex-wife's attorney or to the Court made any difference. Truth, facts, evidence or even the best interest of my children had no affect on the outcome. The family court system is broken, but from my experience, it is not the laws, it's the lawyers. They feed off of the conflict. They are not hired to reduce conflict or protect the best interest of children, which is why third parties need to be involved. It should be mandatory for children to have a guardian ad litem, with extensive training in abuse and aggression.

It is absolutely shameful that the Fairfax County Court did nothing to intervene or understand the ongoing conflict. Judge Randy Bellows also used the children as punishment, by withholding access for failing to fax a receipt. The entire conflict centered around the denial of access to the children, it was inconceivable to me that he would use children like this. This is exactly what my ex-wife was doing and now Judge Bellows was doing it for her. To all my family, friends and the people that supported me through this process, I am so sorry. I know my reactions and behavior throughout this process did not always make sense. None of this made sense to me either. I had no help and the only suggestion I got from my attorneys was to remain silent. At first, I did what I was told, remained silent and listened to my attorneys. Then after I had given my ex-wife full custody to try and appease her, I learned about Psychopathy and emailed Dr. Samenow about my concerns and asked him for help. Of course,

I was ignored.

As the conflict continued, I was forced to defend myself. When that didn't work, I thought I could get the help I needed by speaking out. There is no right or wrong way to defend yourself from abuse. Naively, I thought that abuse was abuse and it would be recognized and something would be done. I thought speaking out would end the abuse or at least get them to back off.

It didn't. When no one did anything they were emboldened.

I took my own life because I had come to the conclusion that there was nothing I could do or say to end the abuse. Every time I got up off my knees, I would get knocked back down. They were not going to let me be the father I wanted to be to my children. People may think I am a coward for giving up on my children, but I didn't see how I was going to heal from this. I have no money for an attorney, therapy or medication. I have lost 4 jobs because of this process. I was going to be at their mercy for the rest of my life and they had shown me none. Being alienated, legally abused, emotionally abused, isolated and financially ruined are all a recipe for suicide. I wish I were stronger to keep going, but the emotional pain and fear of going to court and jail became overwhelming. I became paralyzed with fear.

I couldn't flee and I could not fight. I was never going to be allowed to heal or recover. I wish I were better at articulating the

> *psychological and emotional trauma I experienced. I could fill a book with all the lies and mysterious rulings of the Court. Never have I experienced this kind of pain. I asked for help, but good men did nothing and evil prevailed. All I wanted was a Guardian Ad Litem for my children. Any third party would have been easily been able to confirm or refute all of my allegations, which is why none was ever appointed to protect the children or reduce the conflict.*
>
> *Abuse is about power and control. Stand up for the abused and speak out. If someone speaks out about abuse, believe them. Please teach my children empathy and about emotional invalidation and 'gas-lighting' or they may end up like me.*
>
> *God have mercy on my soul"*

Now, I haven't read his family court file, nor am I privy to any of the facts contained in this man's case. I cannot verify the veracity of his statements. However, the fact that his ex-wife sought to copyright the suicide note to explicitly prevent others from discovering the information contained therein leads me to believe this note should be given, at least, some credibility.

With that said, I believe the gender-biased family court system created by feminism's war on marriage is responsible for not only the death of this man, but many others who didn't have the emotional fortitude to pen such a note before killing themselves.

Again, this is another example of feminism's sexist war on marriage and its catastrophic consequences on men. Thanks to feminism, Western society considers men so disposable that even the U.S. government has become complicit in feminism's war on men.

On October 5, 2010, Caroline May, penned an article for the Daily Caller, *"Breast cancer receives much more research funding, publicity than prostate cancer despite similar number of victims."* Her article cites the following estimates from the U.S. National Institute of Health,

> *"2010, 207,090 women and 1,970 men will get new cases of breast cancer, while 39,840 women and 390 men will likely die from the disease. The estimated new cases of prostate cancer this year — all affecting men — is 217,730, while it is predicted 32,050 will die from the disease."*

When May interviewed The Prostate Cancer Foundation's V.P of Communication Dan Zenka, he said,

> *"Prostate cancer is to men what breast cancer is to women."*

What was the U.S. Government's response? May tells us,

> *"Breast cancer awareness advocates have done an inspired job getting out word and excitement for their cause. Despite their success, prostate cancer has been left in the dust — both in terms of awareness and federal funding. Case in point, prostate cancer research receives less than half of the funding breast cancer does.*
>
> *In fiscal year 2009, breast cancer research received $872 million worth of federal funding, while prostate cancer received $390 million. It is estimated that fiscal year 2010 will end similarly, with breast cancer research getting $891 million and prostate*

cancer research receiving $399 million."

While May's article makes it clear that breast cancer receives both more attention and funding, critics might argue that by itself, that doesn't mean the U.S. government views men as disposable. Frankly, I agree, which is why I looked deeper into the issue. What I found was striking.

To prove exactly how much the United States is committed to gender equality, one needs to look no farther than the internet. If the reader goes to their internet browser on either their smartphone, tablet, or computer and they type in the internet address: *www.womenshealth.gov*, it brings the reader to a woman's health website sponsored by the U.S. government that includes both women's health information and resources.

If the reader types in *www.menshealth.gov*, at the time of this writing, that website doesn't even exist.

That should tell you everything you need to know about how much both feminism and the U.S. government care about men's health and well-being.

While feminism and its followers claim they're being victimized by men and misogyny, the facts make it clear the reality is that feminist ideology is persecuting men and families, while destroying our communities in the process.

Remember this the next time some idiot tells you that feminism is about gender equality.

4 THE WAGE GAPE LIE

It seems like almost monthly the mainstream media, feminist activists, and feminist scholars have told everyone within earshot there's a wage gap between men and women. Further, they claim that because women are discriminated against in employment wages, they need more protections. To support their views, they conduct studies, surveys, and other forms of "scholarly" research to prove the validity of their claims.

However, it's all a lie. If one ever needed an example of fake news, the mainstream reporting on the wage gap serves as a textbook example. Almost all major media outlets are guilty of it.

Now I know this seems a bold statement, but this lie has been so far-reaching that it's appropriate to soapbox for an entire chapter, providing incontrovertible facts and analysis to prove the intellectual dishonesty of this argument.

Full disclosure: I can't debunk the wage gap lie. This is

because history already did that for me. Specifically, the Equal Protection Act of 1963, signed by U.S. President Kennedy. The Equal Pay Act (EPA) made it illegal nationwide for employers to discriminate against women for wages.

When the Act was signed, President John F. Kennedy remarked, in pertinent part,

> *"I am delighted today to approve the Equal Pay Act of 1963, which prohibits arbitrary discrimination against women in the payment of wages. This Act represents many years of effort by labor, management, and several private organizations unassociated with labor or management, to call attention to the unconscionable practice of paying female employees less wages than male employees for the same jobs. This measure adds to our laws another structure basic to democracy. It will add protection at the working place to the women, the same rights at the working place in a sense that they have enjoyed at the polling place.*
>
> *I am grateful to those members of Congress who worked so diligently to guide the Equal Pay Act through. It affirms our determination that women enter the labor force, they will find equality in their pay envelopes."*

You see, this feminist fight for equal pay was won over half a century ago. So to those feminists and their useful idiots who perpetuate this blatant lie, I have to say, *"The history is clear, please stop lying."*

Now I'll spend the rest of this chapter adding insult to injury. You're welcome.

The Equal Employment Opportunities Commission, one of the governmental authorities tasked with enforcing this decades-old law makes the law clear,

> *" The Equal Pay Act requires that men and women be given equal pay for equal work in the same establishment. The jobs need not be identical, but they must be substantially equal. It is job content, not job titles, that determines whether jobs are substantially equal. Specifically, the EPA provides that employers may not pay unequal wages to men and women who perform jobs that require substantially equal skill, effort and responsibility, and that are performed under similar working conditions within the same establishment."*

Further, they break it down even more and describe the factors they consider, including, but not limited to: skill, effort, responsibility and working conditions.

Skill is measured by,

> *"Factors such as the experience, ability, education, and training required to perform the job. The issue is what skills are required for the job, not what skills the individual employees may have. For example, two bookkeeping jobs could be considered equal under the EPA even if one of the job holders has a master's degree in physics, since that degree would not be required for the job."*

Effort is measured factors such as,

> *"The amount of physical or mental exertion needed to perform the job. For example, suppose that men and women work side by*

> *side on a line assembling machine parts. The person at the end of the line must also lift the assembled product as he or she completes the work and place it on a board. That job requires more effort than the other assembly line jobs if the extra effort of lifting the assembled product off the line is substantial and is a regular part of the job. As a result, it would not be a violation to pay that person more, regardless of whether the job is held by a man or a woman."*

Responsibility is measured by,

> *"The degree of accountability required in performing the job. For example, a salesperson who is delegated the duty of determining whether to accept customers' personal checks has more responsibility than other salespeople. On the other hand, a minor difference in responsibility, such as turning out the lights at the end of the day, would not justify a pay differential."*

Working Conditions are determined by,

> *"two factors: (1) physical surroundings like temperature, fumes, and ventilation; and (2) hazards."*

However, this isn't the entirety of the factors considered when determining whether someone is discriminated against for purposes of this law. They also allow differences in pay based on the following,

> *"seniority, merit, quantity or quality of production, or a factor other than sex."*

What does this mean?

It means that even if a woman has the same job title as a man, if that man has more experience, training, skill, responsibility, or he's a better worker who puts in more effort and produces better and a higher quality product than his female co-worker with the same job title, he gets more money.

Just because a woman works at a job making less money doesn't mean she's entitled to more. Like anyone else, she should earn it. You see, equal opportunity only means women get on the same playing field as a man. After that she has to prove her work ethic, knowledge, experience, and training are equal to that of her male counterparts to be legally entitled to equal wages.

The question I have to ask feminists is: Why aren't you educating your followers on this very simple to understand law? I cannot perceive a single ethical reason why a feminist organization would purposefully keep their followers ignorant of something so life changing as this decades-old victory.

Now I can see feminists responding that even though the law's on the books, it's not being enforced and the wage gap still exists.

The most credible studies and facts show that while a wage gap exists, it's between about 4% to 7%, after you correct for side by side comparisons based on experience, job requirements, training, and skill levels. This is well within scientific error of plus or minus 5%. Most objective and credible researchers consider a variation within this range as negligible.

Now this isn't just me making spurious unsupported statements. These views are shared by Christina Hoff Sommers. She's a feminist scholar whose views are dictated by the facts and not dogmatic ideologies.

Christina has her PhD in philosophy and was a professor at the University of Massachusetts, and later an associate professor at Clark University. Afterward, she became a W.H. Brady fellow at the American Enterprise Institute. She's an author of many books and created and produces an online video series, "*The Factual Feminist.*" She's also a member of the Board of Advisors for the Foundation for Individual Rights in Education, and received an award from the National Women's Political Caucus for Exceptional Merit in Media in 2013. As of 2014, she's also a registered Democrat.

In her November 4, 2012, article for the Huffington Post, she debunks the wage gap myth using the Association of University Women's study, "*Graduating to a Pay Gap.*" She states the hard numbers within this study show the 23 cent difference between men and women is demonstratively proven to be a reflection of the difference between raw earnings between men and women employed full time. However, once the figures are adjusted to control for the relevant variables the wage gap practically vanishes.

Then she goes on to cite the U.S. Department of Labor's meta-study where they examined over 50 peer-reviewed papers where the Department of Labor concluded that the wage gap,

> "*...may be almost entirely the result of individual choices being made by both male and female workers*".

What's interesting is that while feminists do their best to personally attack Hoff-Sommers, no one ever credibly questions her research or sources. In fact, they're so busy making personal attacks against her, none of her positions has ever been legitimately challenged.

Further, her view is supported by the Department of Labor. On January 12, 2009, the U.S. Department of Labor published a 95-page report entitled, "*An Analysis of the Reasons for the Disparity in Wages Between Men and Women.*" Right in the beginning of the report, the Department of Labor Deputy Assistant Secretary for Federal Contract Compliance Charles E. James Sr. states,

> "*During the past three decades, women have made notable gains in the workplace and in pay equity, including increased labor force participation, substantial gains in educational attainment, employment growth in higher paying occupations, and significant gains in real earnings.*
>
> *However, despite these gains the raw wage gap continues to be used in misleading ways to advance public policy agendas without fully explaining the reasons behind the gap.*"

In case you missed it, saying that the raw numbers have been misleading is the politically correct way of saying that feminists are being dishonest about the wage gap to further their feminist political agenda.

To be even more clear, feminists are lying.

Why would this Department of Labor official make such a damning statement? The answer to this question is in the report itself, which made the following conclusion:

> "*Economic research has identified many factors that account for portions of the gender wage gap. Some of the factors are consequences of differences in decisions made by women and men in balancing their work, personal, and family lives.*"

Noticeably absent from the report was any conclusion that the wage gap existed because of any kind of patriarchal oppression or any other of the ideological myths perpetuated by feminist lies. In fact, this author cannot find any credible study or research conducted by a non-feminist ideologue that supports the idea the wage gap is caused by discrimination against women.

As long as feminists continue lying about the wage gap, they'll continue to like liars and idiots every time they bring it up.

5 THE FAKE RAPE PANDEMIC

> "Rape exists any time sexual intercourse occurs when it has not been initiated by the woman"
> -Robin Morgan, Ms. Magazine

Merriam Webster defines a pandemic as,

> *"an outbreak of a disease that occurs over a wide geographic area and affects an exceptionally high proportion of the population."*

While there were many pandemics throughout history, the European Black Plague is one of the most notable. Historians date Black Plague outbreaks in Asia as early as 1338 in what is now Kyrgyzstan. It eventually moved to Europe around 1346 and killed between 70 million and 100 million people. This represents 45% to 50% of Europe's population at the time or to put it in simpler terms, it killed 1 in 2 Europeans. Think about it, a disease so deadly that half of everyone you know dies, your friends, family, coworkers, neighbors...everyone.

To say it devastated European society is a major understatement. The survivors were so terrified they persecuted anyone different from them from lepers and beggars to foreigners. As an extreme example, their terror was so great there were reports that they executed people with Acne and Psoriasis, fearing these people were plague carriers.

In 1918, there was a global flu pandemic that infected around 500 million people worldwide. It killed somewhere upwards of 100 million people or 20 % of those infected. At the time, these deaths represented 3% to 5% of the world's population. Even the survivors, who were merely infected, experienced symptoms so severe that many were either completely incapacitated or nearly incapacitated. Businesses closed and entire communities were devastated because they were too sick to take care of themselves.

In 1981 the American public became aware of the AIDS and HIV pandemic. On June 5th, 1981 the United States CDC (Centers for Disease Control) published in their Morbidity and Mortality Weekly Report a description of a rare lung infection called Pneumocystis Carinii Pneumonia (PCP) infecting young healthy gay men. This is the first official report of the AIDS epidemic.

Within days of publishing the original June 5th, 1981 report, major news outlets picked up the story and doctors across the country started flooding the CDC with reports of cases of infection that were similar. By the end of the year, 270 people were identified as being infected and of those, 121 had died. September 24th, 1982, was the date the CDC first used the term AIDS (acquired immune deficiency syndrome) to describe this illness.

Again, like other pandemics, people became terrified and so, as with many pandemics before, those not infected started persecuting those around them.

As an example, in 1987, Ricky Ray, a 15-year-old HIV positive hemophiliac, fought in Federal Court for the right for him and his HIV-positive siblings to attend public school. The Federal Court found in their favor and after they were reinstated in school, they were subjected to boycotts by people in their community. This eventually led to their family home being burnt to the ground on August 28th, 1987. Ray died in 1992. He is only one of many cases where those infected with HIV/AIDS virus were discriminated against by others around them.

By 1994, AIDS became the leading cause of death for all Americans aged 25-44. However, in 1996, two years later, the CDC reported that this was no longer the case for Americans in this age group. As of 2014, WHO (World Health Organization) estimates there are close to 37 million people worldwide infected with HIV. WHO estimates that one in eight people infected is unaware they even have HIV.

According to RAINN (Rape Abuse & Incest National Network), 1 out of every 6 women in the United States has been the victim of either rape or attempted rape in her lifetime. According to RAINN, this means approximately 17% of all women in the United States are rape victims. On September 21, 2015 American Association of Universities issued a report, based on a survey, that found that 1 in 4 women attending college are sexually assaulted.

Even though rape is a crime in Western and modern societies and not a disease, feminists report it as though it were a some kind of pandemic result of rape culture. If the above stats were accurate, they'd be right.

However, the facts debunk this lie as well.

Like all other modern and civilized societies, rape and sexual assault in the United States are considered crimes.

With that in mind, we must necessarily consider also that in the United States, one of the most sacred principles in our justice system is a legal presumption that people accused of a crime are legally considered innocent until proven guilty. This legal presumption of innocence was codified in the US legal system in the 1895 US Supreme Court case, *Coffin v. United States*. Nolo's Plain English Law Dictionary paraphrases the Supreme Court's definition as,

> *"One of the most sacred principles in the American criminal justice system, holding that a defendant is innocent until proven guilty. In other words, the prosecution must prove, beyond a reasonable doubt, each essential element of the crime charged."*

Additionally, in criminal court, a rape suspect also has the right to confront their accuser and be judged by a jury of their peers. They're even given the right to have an attorney represent them. If they cannot afford an attorney themselves, the courts will provide one free of charge.

These rights aren't just for rape suspects, these rights apply to every United States citizen accused of a crime.

Criminal conviction is how US citizens determine whether someone is a criminal or, in this case, whether someone is a rapist.

Like any other crime, rape and sexual assault statistics

are tracked by the United States Government. Specifically, the FBI (Federal Bureau of Investigation) and the BJS (Bureau of Justice Statistics) are two of the agencies that record and maintain records on a variety of types of crime reported by various local law enforcement agencies throughout the country. These agencies then use this information to develop statistics for national crime trends. More importantly, they break down the statistics and trends for each type of crime reported to them. They then release this information to the public annually.

Prior to 2013, the FBI's definition of rape under the UCR (uniform crime reporting) was,

> *"The carnal knowledge of a female forcibly and against her will."*

However, 2013, the FBI changed the way it defined rape and started to collect rape data under the revised definition. Beginning with the 2013 data year, the term *"forcible"* was removed from the title of the crime and the definition was changed. The revised UCR definition of rape is now:

> *"Penetration, no matter how slight, of the vagina or anus with any body part or object, or oral penetration by a sex organ of another person, without the consent of the victim."*

Further, attempted rapes or assaults to commit rape are now also included under this new definition.

While RAINN and other feminist organizations allege women are raped and sexually assaulted at pandemic levels across the country, the official United States government data directly and drastically debunks these allegations.

The facts couldn't contradict the feminist narrative more clearly.

The FBI reports the rate of rape and sexual assault per 100,000 people in the United States. In 1995, 37.1 women out of every 100,000 reported being raped under the old definition.

When the definition of rape changed in 2013, the rate of rape reporting to law enforcement increased under the new definition by about 10 per 100,000 people for 2013 and 2014. With this in mind, we can reasonably extrapolate and conclude that the actual number of rapes reported to law enforcement in 1995, if we used the expanded 2013 definition, was probably closer to 47.1 per 100,000 citizens, rather than the 37.1 under the old definition.

However, feminists always argue that rape is a crime that's drastically under reported in the United States. Their view is actually supported by The BJS (Bureau of Justice Statistics). The special report compiled by the United States BJS entitled: "*Female Victims of Sexual Violence, 1994-2010*" released in March 2013, states:

> "*In 1995, 29% of rape or sexual assault victimizations against females were reported to police. This percentage increased to 56% in 2003 before declining to 35% in 2010.*"

Even though the United States legal system operates under the principle of innocent until proven guilty, the stance that feminists take is that every time a woman claims someone raped her, the accused assailant is automatically presumed guilty until proven innocent. This view directly opposes the long-held American legal principle of innocent until proven guilty.

The March 2013 report compiled by the BJS takes the feminist view of guilty until proven innocent. It assumes every time a woman reports she was raped or sexually assaulted, that a crime actually occurred and that the person she accused is guilty, without the benefit of being charged with a crime, or the benefit of a guilty conviction after a criminal trial.

Unfortunately, The BJS report is the closest thing to objective reporting we have on the subject, so absent a more objective source, we're forced to use it. With that in mind, if we extrapolate from BJS report, based on 1995 data above, 71% of rapes weren't reported to law enforcement.

Given that we previously concluded that if the new 2013 FBI definition of rape had been used in 1995, approximately 47.1 rapes per 100,000 people would've been reported. Now if we incorporate the BJS under-reporting findings, In 1995, the 47.1 number only represents 29% of the actual amount of sexual assaults committed (assuming all suspects were guilty). Therefore, assuming that every one of these reports was a legitimate report of rape and that the suspect identified was actually guilty, 115.3 rapes per 100,000 were committed and weren't reported.

Then when added to the original number of 47.1, this brings the amount of rapes committed against women in 1995 to 162.4 rapes per 100,000 people, again this assumes ever rape report was an honest report and that the suspect accused was actually guilty of the crime.

Now let's use these same numbers and merge them into what we know from 2014. The 2014 FBI rape trend report documented 36.6 rapes per 100,000 people. As we previously discussed, this only represents 29% of all rapes in 2014. Now if all rapes were reported, according to the BJS report, the number would increase to 126.2 rapes per 100,000 people occurring in 2014, again, using the 1995 BJS under-reporting percentages.

When you look objectively at the United States Government official statistics and correcting for under-reporting, only 0.2%, or two-tenths of one percent of women have been raped, and that's rounding up. It's actually less than that. It's closer to 0.16%. Again, this is assuming that every time a woman reports a rape, the suspect is already presumed guilty.

Now, remember, these numbers merely represent the number of accusations of rape reported and concluded to be under-reported. These numbers do not represent the number of men actually determined by a criminal court to be guilty.

They're just the initial reports. So of those reports, how many of these suspected rapists are arrested?

According to the FBI, in 2014, after conducting an investigation, The FBI found that law enforcement obtained enough evidence to arrest suspects in only 38% to 39% of the rapes reported to them.

If you look at this from the *"innocent until proven guilty"* legal standard, then between 61% and 62% of all rapes or sexual assaults reported to law enforcement aren't credible enough to make an arrest, let alone criminally prosecute.

Remember, this is after a criminal investigation is completed.

Let that sink in for a moment.

Using the American legal standard of "innocent until proven guilty," this proves that the FBI found that at least 61%, or 3 in 5, of all rape accusations reported to the police, are false.

The FBI's findings are anecdotally confirmed by Bingham County, Idaho Sheriff Craig Rowland. In March 2016, Sheriff Rowland was interviewed and publicly stated,

> *"The majority of our rapes that are called in, are actually consensual sex."*

As a law enforcement agency, the Sheriff's office investigates rape and sexual assault, and are experts in the field of criminal investigation. Thus law enforcement officials, having the most experience and training, are in the best position to give an expert opinion.

More importantly, the science not only supports high levels of false rape allegations, it further identifies why women make up false rape allegations in the first place.

Eugene J. Kanin PhD of Purdue University's Department of Sociology and Anthropology, conducted a nine-year case study entitled: *"False Rape Allegations."* It was published in the Archives of Sexual Behavior Vol 23, No.1, in 1994. The Archives of Sexual Behavior is the official publication of the Academy of Sex Research and is an accredited peer-reviewed academic journal in sexology established in 1971.

The Kanin study was limited in scope in that it focused on rapes that were reported to have actually occurred...not attempted rapes that failed. The police department Dr. Kanin chose for the study took a very novel approach to determine whether a rape allegation was false. In each instance, before the rape allegation was conclusively found to be a lie, the law enforcement agency required the woman to voluntarily sign a declaration, under penalty of perjury, admitting she made a false accusation of rape. If the female rape accuser refused to sign the declaration, neither the study nor the law enforcement agency considered her rape accusation a false report. As such, Dr. Kanin found it to be the perfect testing ground for studying false rape allegations.

Dr. Kanin's study found that 41% of all rape reports studied were confirmed false. Now since this study was over a period of nine years, it also tracked false rape reporting rates year to year, and found that in some years, false rape reports occurred as little as 23% of the time, but skyrocketed in other years to 70%.

In addition to determining what percentage of women lied about being raped, the study collected enough information to discover the main reasons women use for making a false accusation of rape. The study found that women lied about rape for three main purposes.

Approximately 56% of false rape allegations were to serve as an alibi to cover up a consensual sexual encounter. Dr. Kanin notes the following example from the study,

> *"A married 30 year old female reported that she had been raped in her apartment complex. During polygraph examination, she admitted she was a willing partner. She reported she had been raped because her partner did not stop before ejaculation, as he had agreed, and she was afraid she was pregnant. Her husband was overseas."*

About 27% of false rape allegations were used as a means for the woman to exact revenge because the man rejected her. An example Dr. Kanin noted follows,

> "An 18 year old woman was having sex with a boarder in her mother's house for a period of 3 months. When the mother learned of her behavior from other boarders, the mother ordered the man to leave. The complainant learned that her lover was packing and she went to his room and told him she was ready to leave with him in an hour. He responded with "who the hell wants you." She briefly argued with him and then proceeded to the police station to report that he had raped her. She admitted the false charge during the polygraph examination."

Finally, close to 18% of false rape allegations were for attention seeking and sympathy purposes. Dr. Kanin notes,

> "An unmarried female, age 41, was in postdivorce counseling, and she wanted more attention and sympathy from her counselor because she "liked him." She fabricated a rape episode, and he took her to the police station and assisted her in making the charge. She could not back out because she would have to admit to lying to him. She admitted the false allegation when she was offered to be polygraphed."

What the Kanin study confirms is that weighing the credibility of witnesses and alleged victims is absolutely necessary, not only to solve rape crimes, but also to discover whether a crime actually occurred. Law enforcement is specially trained for this function.

This isn't victim blaming, this is common sense. Remember, innocent until proven guilty. Not, guilty until proven innocent.

Now we've reviewed the FBI rape arrest statistics and the Kanin Study of the prevalence of false rape accusations, let's compare this with the FBI's rape reporting statistics. Let's look at both 1995 and 2014 again.

In using the information above, we know that for 1995, only 63.2 cases per 100,000 people were found by law enforcement to be credible enough to make an arrest. Again, this is after correcting for under-reporting of rape based on the BJS's own numbers.

In 2014, using this same methodology, this means that 48.6 rape reports per 100,000 people would have been found after an investigation credible enough to make an arrest.

When Kanin's findings are incorporated, we know that about 41% of those men accused of rape were arrested for a crime they didn't commit. For 1995, this means that 25 men were arrested for a crime they didn't commit. In 2014, 19 men were arrested for a crime they didn't commit.

These men were innocent victims of false rape accusations.

Why is this important?

It's important because women are allowed falsely accuse a man of rape and destroy his life with little to no recourse. Innocent men have been attacked, murdered and committed suicide because of false rape allegations.

As the following examples demonstrate, this isn't hyperbole.

In 1955, a 14-year-old African-American Mississippi boy, Emmett Louis Till, was brutally tortured and lynched after a married woman, Carolyn Bryant, accused him of wolf whistling her and attempted sexual assault. Till was brutally kidnapped, tortured and eventually murdered by Bryant's husband and others.

Six decades later, Carolyn Bryant admitted to Professor Timothy B. Tyson in his book, *"The Blood of Emmett Till,"* that she lied about Till attempting to sexually assault her.

Bryant's lie inspired a vigilante mob to torture and murder a 14-year-old child.

Emmett Till was innocent.

In 2009, John Keogh, a diagnosed mental health patient, was accused by a fellow hospital patient of raping her. The police interviewed him on July 1, 2009. Based on their interview and investigation, they cleared Keogh as a suspect on July 4, 2009. However, the police never told him he was no longer considered a suspect.

Keogh was so distraught over being falsely accused of rape that he hung himself. His body was found in his hospital room bathroom on July 7, 2009.

John Keogh was innocent.

On January 10, 2009, WRCB TV reported that Dalton, Georgia police officer Robert Paul Sparks, a 10-year veteran of the department, was accused by a woman of raping her. Apparently, officer Sparks was responding to a fight at the Oyster Pub and the accuser, who was apparently involved in the fight, claimed to not have her ID on her. She and Sparks returned to her hotel, the Guest Inn, presumably to get her ID.

While she originally claimed he raped her, when she was brought to the police station, she later admitted she lied and that the sex was consensual. Officer Sparks was notified of the accusation and called back to the station. Before he could be told the accusation was false, he shot himself in the head in the police station bathroom.

The Dalton Police Department later released the following statement,

> *"An investigation into a reported January 10, 2009 sexual assault by the Georgia Bureau of Investigation and reviewed by the Conasauga Judicial Circuit District Attorney's Office has found no evidence of criminal wrongdoing by the late Dalton Police Department Officer Paul Sparks. The District Attorney's Office has also concluded that while it is clear that the complainant made false statements to investigators, there's insufficient evidence to support criminal charges for making false statements to investigators.*
>
> *At approximately 1:30 AM on January 10, officers from the Dalton Police Department responded to a report of a fight between two females at the Oyster Pub Bar at 2206 Chattanooga Road. One of the females was gone when officers arrived at the scene, but she was later contacted by Officer Paul Sparks when she returned to the bar to pay her bar tab. According to the investigation, Sparks asked for the complainant's identification which she'd left back in Room 128 at the Guest Inn. Sparks apparently followed her to her room to get the ID, continuing to ask questions about the fight.*
>
> *At approximately 3:00 AM, two of the complainant's friends met her at the Guest*

Inn and reportedly found her crying and upset. After speaking to her, one of these men called 911 at approximately 3:22 AM to report a sexual assault by a Dalton Police Officer. The supervising sergeant on duty was dispatched and responded to the scene at approximately 3:30 AM and began an investigation. The complainant's friends told the sergeant that the complainant was raped by a Dalton Police Officer, but the complainant only confirmed that they'd had intercourse. Detectives were called to the scene at approximately 3:55 AM. At approximately 4:00 AM, the shift supervisor contacted Officer Sparks and told him to report to the Police Services Center at 301 Jones Street and wait there with another officer. Officer Sparks arrived at 4:14 AM. At approximately 4:25, the complainant left the scene with a female deputy from the Whitfield County Sheriff's Office, who was the only available female on-duty law enforcement officer, and taken to Hamilton Medical Center to be examined by a Sexual Assault Nurse Examiner (SANE).

While members of the department's command staff discussed the case and how to proceed in the Criminal Investigation Division wing of the Police Services Center, Officer Sparks excused himself into the bathroom in the Patrol Division wing sometime around 5:30 AM. At approximately 5:40 AM, Officer Sparks used his department-issued Sig 40-caliber hand gun to shoot himself once in the head in a shower stall in the Patrol Division bathroom, killing himself. He was later

*pronounced dead at Hamilton Medical
Center. Investigators did not have an
opportunity to speak to Officer Sparks about
the case, and he had not been provided any
details of the allegations.*

*At this point, assistance was requested from
the Georgia Bureau of Investigation, with
the Dalton Police Department cooperating
in support of the investigation.*

*Before being examined at Hamilton Medical
Center by a SANE nurse, the complainant
was interviewed by the nurse. She told the
nurse that she had a sexual encounter with
Officer Sparks, and that the encounter was
completely consensual. During the same
pre-exam interview, she said the officer
indicated to her that he could take her to jail
for her involvement in the fight. In an
interview later that morning with agents of
the GBI and DPD, the complainant repeated
that the encounter was consensual but told
investigators that the officer said he could
take her to jail and that the other woman in
the fight could press charges. She said that
the encounter was consensual, stating that
at no point did Officer Sparks threaten,
command, or force her to have sex and that
the officer did not instruct her not to talk
about what happened. As part of this
examination, the SANE nurse completed a
sexual assault kit that was sent to the GBI
Crime Lab for analysis.*

*During the course of several interviews with
investigators from the DPD and the GBI,
the complainant's story changed several
times, at one point telling investigators that*

only oral sex was involved, but in these interviews she never changed the fact that the encounter was consensual.

An examination of the sexual assault kit at the GBI Crime Lab indicated the presence of male DNA, but the amount was insufficient to identify whose DNA it was. The crime lab chemist indicated that this could be due to the sample being "old" from a previous sexual encounter, or that the male donor had a vasectomy at some point, which Officer Sparks had 22 years ago. Other tests at the GBI Crime Lab, including DNA and hair samples from both the officer and the complainant failed to produce any evidence that a sexual encounter had occurred. The District Attorney's Office concluded that physical evidence in the case does not prove a sexual encounter happened, but that it also does not preclude a sexual encounter.

The District Attorney's Office concluded that there is no evidence that Officer Sparks committed a rape, a violation of OCGA 16-6-1 which defines Rape as "carnal knowledge of: (1) a female forcibly and against her will". While the DA's Office states that while there may have been an inducement, even by Sparks' authority as a law enforcement officer, that inducement would be insufficient to be "against her will".

The District Attorney's Office also concluded that there is insufficient evidence that Sparks' actions would have been a violation of OCGA 16-6-5.1: "Sexual Assault Against Persons In Custody".

Section (c)(1) states:

"A person commits sexual assault when such person has supervisory or disciplinary authority over another person and such other person engages in sexual contact with that other person who is: (A) in custody of the law...".

While the complainant was not under arrest at any point, the District Attorney concludes that it could be argued she was "in custody of the law", and therefore any encounter could violate this statute. However, the District Attorney's Office found that a lack of credibility of the complainant and the crime lab results make it impossible to prove that any encounter actually happened.

The District Attorney's Office also found insufficient evidence to charge the complainant with violation of OCGA 16-10-20, which makes it a crime to make a false statement to police. While the DA found that it was clear false statements were made, based on the contradictory statements made to investigators, it is impossible to prove which statements are true, if any, and which are false.

"This is a serious case that has permanently altered the lives of everyone involved," Chief Parker said upon completion of the investigation. "I want citizens to know that we take these kinds of allegations seriously, and will exhaust every resource to get to the truth; the public's trust is not something we take for granted – we know that it is earned.

> *But I also want our officers to know that we have and will always wait until all the facts are in before making conclusions. We appreciate the assistance of the Georgia Bureau of Investigation and the District Attorney's Office in this case; their involvement adds considerable weight to the findings."*
>
> *The investigation into this incident by both the Georgia Bureau of Investigation and the Dalton Police Department is closed."*

Officer Sparks was innocent.

On June 2, 2010, the Daily Mail reported that 27-year-old Olumide Fadayomi was cleared of raping a UK woman. Leading up to his trial, Mr. Fadayomi admitted he lost his home, close friends, and his job. His trial lasted only 45 minutes before Sheffield Crown Judge Patrick Robertshaw cleared him.

Even more disturbing was that Judge Robertshaw expressed concern that the prosecution was biased against Mr. Fadayomi. You see, the woman who accused Mr. Fadayomi of rape had a history of lying about being raped in the past. Four years previously, she accused a 21-year-old man, Daniel Devennie, of rape. 18 months after he was first arrested, he took his own life.

Both Devennie and Fadayomi were innocent. But they both suffered tragically because of one woman's lie.

They were innocent.

In January 2013, the Telegraph reported about the murder of 18-year-old Luke Harwood. He was falsely accused of rape by Alice Hall. Hall reported her accusation to the police. They investigated and determined she had not been raped. In other words, she lied about being raped. After being cleared of charges, Hall's sister Emma and a gang of four of Emma's friends brutally beat Harwood to death. They kicked him and stomped on his head until he died.

Luke Harwood was innocent.

On March 2014, the Daily Mail reported that 16-year-old teenager, Tom Acton, was harassed and bullied into taking ecstasy, amphetamines and cocaine by his classmates at Poynton High School and Performing Arts College. Acton reported it to the school officials who did nothing about it.

As a result of the constant harassment, his mother removed him from the school, rumors began circulating that he tied a girl up to a tree, raped her, and took pictures of it. The rumors spread and he was repeatedly harassed and beaten by mobs of up to 30 other youths telling he and his family they wanted to kill him.

He was so depressed he started carving rapist into his leg. Shortly before he was to testify against one of his assailants, who beat him and held a knife to his throat, he was found hanged in his bedroom. He'd committed suicide.

One of his assailants, Thomas Greenwood, later admitted to a court to assaulting Tom. Also, a math teacher at Tom's former school, Fatimah Ahmed, pled guilty to concealing, disguising, converting, transferring or removing criminal property related to drug money that flowed through her bank account.

Tom hanged himself because he was falsely branded a rapist to destroy his credibility.

Tom Acton was innocent.

In January 2015, the Alaska Dispatch News reported that Dominique Vasquez cheated on her boyfriend Abraham Stine, with his cousin, Wesley Lord. After she and Lord had consensual sex, Vasquez got two of Lord's friends, Jeffrey Bodfish and Tyrone Akpik, to falsely believe she'd been raped. A short time later, they unwittingly told Stine that she'd been raped by Lord.

Stine violently beat Lord to death. Vasquez admitted that while Stine brutally and mercilessly beat Lord, she held her hand over Lord's mouth to prevent his screams from being heard.

Lord's only crime? He slept with a cheating slut who lied about being raped to her boyfriend to hide her infidelity. It cost him his life.

Wesley Lord was innocent.

I cannot believe it when RAINN or other organizations claim that 16% to 25% of women have been raped. Especially when the United States Government puts the actual number of female rape victims at less than 1% percent, if we drastically estimate upward. Yet, feminists inflate this number over 80 times to come up with their fake 1 in 6 number.

Further, feminists blame this false rape epidemic on the misguided theory that men have created a rape culture that legitimizes the rape of women. However, even RAINN eventually had to admit that Rape Culture theory was a lie.

On February 28, 2014, RAINN President Scott Berkowitz and Vice President of Public Affairs Rebecca O' Conner penned a letter to the White House Task Force to Protect

Women from Sexual Assault, at the United States Department of Justice in their Office on Violence Against Women.

In their letter to the Task Force, Berkowitz and O'Conner admit,

> *"In the last few years, there has been an unfortunate trend towards blaming "rape culture" for the extensive problem of sexual violence on campuses. Rape is caused not by cultural factors but by the conscious decisions, of a small percentage of the community, to commit a violent crime."*

Even though the idea of a male rape culture has been thoroughly debunked, not just by opponents, but by feminists themselves, it's clear feminists continue to lie about its existence to falsely inflate the number of rapes in the United States.

When feminists realized the fact weren't on their side, what did they do?

They moved the goal posts, of course.

Feminists, for decades, have been vastly expanding their definition of rape from the legal definition, used by law enforcement and the FBI, to something completely different through biased surveys engineered to shape public opinion. Now, most sexual contact, even when consensual, under the constantly evolving feminist definition, is considered rape.

Consider the following quotes from prominent feminist leaders:

Catherine MacKinnon said,

> "...I call it rape whenever a woman has sex and feels violated.
>
> ...all heterosexual intercourse is rape because women, as a group, are not strong enough to give meaningful consent."

To MacKinnon, it doesn't matter if the woman was actually raped...only that she feels violated. Further, even if the woman doesn't feel violated, it's still rape because women, being the weaker sex, cannot give consent. Sounds sexist doesn't it?

Catherine Comins said,

> "Men who are unjustly accused of rape can sometimes gain from the experience"

My questions for Ms. Comins are: What do innocent men gain from being brutally tortured and murdered? What do innocent men gain from getting so depressed they commit suicide as a direct result of being falsely accused?

These people are heartless man-hating bigots.

On January 16, 2014, Nicky Vaught, a staff columnist from the NC State University official student newspaper the Technician writes,

> "But as men, we have no right to tell women what rape is. We have no right to weigh in on the logistics of what constitutes rape. Our role is to shut up and stop raping people."

According to Vaught, this means that whatever women decide to call rape should be considered rape? Apparently so.

Lena Dunham, on December 2014, posted to twitter,

> *"The epidemic of campus rape is so self-evident that there's no need to tell the truth about it."*

What makes Dunham's quote so ironic is that in her autobiography, she freely admits to sexually grooming and molesting her sister. She even refers to herself as a predator.

Finally, of course, we have Robin Morgan, who I quoted at the beginning of this chapter,

> *"I claim that rape exists any time sexual intercourse occurs when it has not been initiated by the woman."*

These feminists are considered leaders and voices within the feminist movement. Yet, to them, the common theme is that most sex, even when consensual, is rape.

As you can plainly see, the feminist definition of rape is nowhere near the legal one. Feminists have long known this. In response, they've pressured courts and colleges to create their own civil rape tribunals to wrongly convict men accused of rape under far lower evidentiary standards.

In short, they've started witch hunting.

Doing this denies men their constitutional due process right to a criminal trial by a jury of their peers, their right to have an attorney present to defend them, their right to meaningfully confront their accusers, and, most importantly, their constitutional right to remain silent. These kangaroo courts were created to prevent men from meaningfully defending themselves against false rape accusations.

These efforts have paid off in spades.

The feminist created civil rape industry empowers women to make false rape allegations with little to no recourse. Basically, a woman, without filing a criminal complaint with law enforcement, can accuse a man of raping her. She can then have a civil court judge or college internal tribunal hear the case. Then these kangaroo courts, without affording the man his due process constitutional rights and defenses, often find the man civilly guilty of the crime of rape. This often happens with little to no real evidence presented against the man who was falsely accused.

There is no independent investigation of the rape accusations, just a trial based only on her allegations against her alleged rapist. If there is an investigation, the investigators are just witch-hunting ideologues who aren't often trained in proper criminal investigation techniques or best practices adopted by law enforcement. Most of the time, there isn't even a police report. The investigators and judges are often just feminist ideologues confirming their own misandric belief that the man is always guilty. Whether he's innocent never enters the equation.

Further, under the feminist standard, the false rape accuser is often represented by feminist advocates who attend the proceedings with her. They help her prepare her arguments and evidence and often may speak in her defense at the kangaroo court to lend the false image of credibility.

Grant Neil was a promising college athlete and student from Colorado State University-Pueblo. He had consensual sex with his girlfriend. Yet, the college investigated him for rape, not even using a civil court standard of investigation, but rather, their own internal feminist policies. The entire time his girlfriend adamantly and repeatedly stated he never raped her and that their sexual encounters were always consensual. Yet, the college suspended him for years and destroyed his collegiate academic and athletic career.

This man is innocent of rape. The woman he was accused of raping, at all times, denied she was raped. Yet, Grant's life was destroyed anyway. At the time of this writing, Mr. Neal is suing the College and the Department of Education.

Grant Neil was innocent.

Caleb Warner was a junior at the University of North Dakota (UND) and a fraternity member of Phi Delta Theta. In December 2009, he met a young woman, they hit it off and a short while later, had consensual sex. The next morning, she expressed an interest in him being her boyfriend. He remained non-committal. A short time later, she sent him a text telling him never to contact her again.

She then told UND that he raped her, Based on her accusation alone, the college expelled him. The college held a hearing in February 2010. Even though Warner had an attorney present, he wasn't allowed to speak or to cross-examine Warner's accuser. The college found him guilty of rape and he was suspended for three years.

The Grand Forks Police Department was notified and opened a criminal investigation. They discovered Warner's accuser gave different accounts to witnesses and had sent Warner a message after the party asking for sex.

Grand Forks PD determined Warner's accuser lied and in May 2010, she was formally charged with a false information or report to law enforcement officers or security officials, a Class A misdemeanor. After the police issued a warrant for her arrest and she left the University of North Dakota and the state of North Dakota. She never returned. She's still a fugitive from the law.

Maybe the National Organization of Women will give her an award for her bravery like they did false rape accuser Emma Sulkowicz.

However, even though the police found Warner's accuser lied, the college refused to vacate their civil charges and didn't reinstate him for over 19 months.

Warner told Aljazeera News he never got his degree and that he believed that a man's due process ends when they first set foot on a college campus. This lying woman destroyed his life and his college career.

Caleb Warner was innocent.

On January 28, 2016, the Daily Beast reported about Matthew (last name withheld), a student at an unnamed small liberal arts college. He was found guilty by a college tribunal of rape. He was accused of two instances of rape. The first he says was consensual, the second, he states the supposed victim came on to him, and he refused and left. Based on the tone of the story, his accuser appears to be male and Matthew admits he's gay. He stated that the college investigators never contacted most of the witnesses he submitted in his defense. Further, based on the story, there doesn't seem to be any police report filed. He was never charged criminally.

The examples above are a few of many.

In these proceedings, men are denied their civil right to an attorney and a trial by a jury of his peers. Often it's his word against his female accuser. The trial often happens less than a month after the woman files charges against him, giving him next to no time to either respond or mount any meaningful defense against her accusations...which are often never filed with law enforcement.

Further, if the man is found guilty of civil rape, he can still lose his constitutional ability to bear firearms and if he has children with his accuser, as is often the case, be forced to pay for a professional supervisor to see his children. This severely limits his ability to parent his children and always destroys their parent-child bond. The United States Supreme Court decision in *Troxel v. Granville* held that a parent's right to their children under the 14th Amendment is one of the most protected rights in the United States.

By civilly charging and prosecuting a man with a crime instead of filing criminal charges, feminists have engineered a system where men can be falsely accused and convicted of rape without affording the man his constitutional right to an attorney or a trial by his peers or even meaningful time to prepare for such a trial. These are clear violations of a man's due process rights under the United States Constitution and violates the most sacred legal tenet of the presumption of innocence until proven guilty.

Remember, according to the federal government, assuming all criminal suspects are found guilty, rape occurs less than 1/5th of 1% percent of the time. Yet feminists make it sound as though it's a pandemic level disease.

False rape accusations have destroyed men's lives across

the world. These lies have wrongfully imprisoned, killed, and otherwise deprived innocent men of their lives, their constitutional right to own a firearm and the ability to meaningfully parent their children.

The Rape Pandemic is one of the greatest and harmful lies of the feminist movement.

6 DEBUNKING THE DV LIES

The subject of domestic violence almost automatically evokes an image of a man beating his wife with their child in the backdrop of the scene, helplessly watching, tears in the child's eyes.

While it's an extremely emotionally charged image, it's also the one that feminists have been marketing for almost 50 years. In fact, when feminists refer to domestic violence, they almost always paint narratives similar to the one above to punctuate their point and gain support. This narrative is so common today as to be canon in the annals of domestic violence. However, as a book of non-fiction, we're going to stick to facts, not feminist fictions or dishonest propaganda.

With that in mind, lets discuss a domestic violence victim that's received little to no attention in the press. 23-year-old Desiere Rants. Desiere was a homicide victim from Ravensdale, Washington. Desiere baby-sat friends children and was planning to be a nursing assistant. She was close to her family and especially her brother when she was murdered.

What makes Desiere so different from the stories we normally hear about? Desiere was the murder victim of the former Chairwoman of the Federal Way Domestic Violence Task Force Lorraine Netherton (AKA Lorraine Laxton).

Kathleen R. Merrill reported in the King County Journal that Netherton called 911 on Friday, November 22, 2002. Netherton said she was in pursuit of child kidnappers. Five minutes passed and the 911 call disconnected. A short while later Netherton called 911 back. This time she reported she shot the driver of the car she was pursuing. She stated the shooting was in self-defense, and claimed the driver had repeatedly punched and pushed her.

When the police arrived, they found Netherton had two firearms, a 9mm semi-auto handgun and a .44 magnum revolver. Netherton then changed her story from the kidnapping narrative she told the 911 dispatcher to the new narrative that she was serving court papers on the father of the 7-year-old child she earlier claimed was kidnapped.

Turns out the father, William Rants, was in a custody battle with the mother of their children Gwen Rees. A tribal court had previously awarded William custody of their 7-year-old child. The mother, rather than respect the order, went forum shopping, got a family court judge from a different jurisdiction to sign a temporary custody order. This order allowed the court to transfer custody of the child from William and placed her with Rees' friend while Rees entered drug treatment. There is no evidence the judge who signed the temporary order was aware of the tribal court's prior ruling. By the way, for those who don't know, forum shopping is when a court litigant gets an adverse ruling before one judge, then keeps looking for another judge until they can find one to rule in their favor. It's highly unethical.

Netherton told arriving police officers that Desiere hit her with a car door while exiting her vehicle and then continued attacking Netherton. Netherton claims she shot Desiere in self-defense after pistol whipping Desiere didn't deter Desiere's attack.

Fortunately, there were witnesses at the scene.

What actually happened is that William and Desiere were picking up William's child from school and drove home. Gwen and Netherton saw them and followed them home in a separate car. When they arrived at William's home, William and the child ran into the home. Desiere, who was driving, then got out of the car.

Witnesses say when Netherton exited her own vehicle, she already had her 9mm pistol in her hand. When Desiere exited the vehicle, Netherton shot and missed. Then Netherton moved up to the car and shot Desiere point-blank in the chest. Once Desiere fell to the ground, Netherton stood over her and shot at her twice more...execution style. According to news reports, a 1-year-old child was in the car. The police later recovered high-performance 9mm shells from the scene.

When the police investigated, they didn't find any evidence Netherton had been in a fight. Further, once the medical examiners did the autopsy, they didn't find any evidence of a fight on Desiere either. However, they confirmed Desiere had been shot twice, which killed her.

The police arrested Netherton and held her on $500,000 bond. While the prosecutors originally charged

Netherton with 1st-degree murder, they later reduced the charges to 2nd-degree murder, without any explanation.

Netherton, was a former Chairwoman of the Federal Way Domestic Violence Task Force. Task Force members voted her out and ousted her entirely from the organization the prior June, because "her violent temper."

Turns out, Desiere wasn't the first victim of Netherton's firearm violence.

In 1988, Netherton shot Theodore Chomin. Netherton said that he attacked her outside the Pipeline Tavern on S.W. Alaska Street in Seattle, Washington around 1 a.m. on March 23, 1988. She claimed during the attack, he scratched her wrists, then hit her in the head after she supposedly refused his advances. She drew a pistol, aimed for Theodore's face and emptied her revolver.

After she shot him, the police arrived and were only able to confirm that she had very slight scratches on her wrists, which were photographed. Further, even though she described a violent struggle where, at one point, she claims she'd been knocked to the ground, the officers noted her clothing was clean and not torn. There was no evidence to suggest that Chomin knocked her to the ground.

Theodore, on the other hand, states he noticed Netherton outside and she seemed to be having problems with her coat. He merely offered to help her. She responded by shouting obscenities at him and before he could react, she drew a revolver, used both hands to aim and shoot him. He rolled out of the way as she continued firing. The entire time, he pleaded with her to stop. He told police he thought she was trying to murder him.

Even though she shot at him six times, he was only hit once. He required surgery as that bullet had nicked his liver. Had Theodore not tried to dodge and roll away from the shots, he would be dead today.

Earlier, in 1983, during her divorce, documents were discovered that indicated Netherton started carrying firearms in her early 20s. Her ex-husband, Scott Netherton said he never knew his ex-wife to be without a firearm. Scott, had also filed a DV protection order against her because she repeatedly assaulted him. Further, at the murder trial, it came out that Netherton filed numerous DV protection orders against ex-husbands and boyfriends.

Apparently, this was a habit.

Netherton was eventually convicted of Desiere's murder and sentenced to over 20 years in prison.

The reason this story is relevant, is because it demonstrates, in very real terms, that domestic violence isn't just a crime perpetuated by a man against a woman. It can also be a drug-addicted mother or ex-wife who gets others to white knight for her, like in this case. The one thing all the news coverage and everyone else missed was that the mom was never charged as an accomplice to Netherton's crime.

She should have been.

Further, there's significant academic support that debunks the stereotypical idea that domestic violence is limited to a man assaulting a woman.

In May 2007, the peer-reviewed, American Journal of Public Health published a study by Daniel J. Whitaker

PhD, Tadesse Haileyesus MS, Monica Swahn PhD, and Linda S. Saltzman PhD, entitled: *"Differences in Frequency of Violence and Reported Injury Between Relationships with Reciprocal and Nonreciprocal Intimate Partner Violence."*

Even before getting into their study, the authors discuss prior studies and note,

> *"Several studies have found that men and women initiate violence against an intimate partner and approximately the same rate."*

In their study, their findings were drawn from a sampling of about 11,000 participants from the National Longitudinal Study of Adolescent Health and were from 18 to 28 years old.

What they found was striking,

> *"Among violent relationships, nearly half (49,7%) were characterized as reciprocally violent. Women reported a significantly greater proportion of violent relationships that were reciprocal versus non-reciprocal than did men."*

In other words, women were more likely to be in a mutually violent relationship with men, than men being in a mutually violent relationship with women. Further:

> *"Among relationships with non-reciprocal violence, women were reported to be the perpetrator in a majority of cases (70.7%), as reported by both women(67.7%) and men (74.9%)."*

That's right, in relationships where only one party is the domestic violence perpetrator, over 70% of the time, the abuser is the woman.

Just as damning, In September 2014, J.D. Glass reported, in the Advocate, that the *National Violence Against Women Survey* found that women living with same sex-partners experience intimate partner violence in their lifetimes at a rate of 35.4%, whereas heterosexual women experienced it at a rate of 20.4% across their lifetime.

This means that lesbian women were 75% more likely to be victims of domestic violence than heterosexual women. Further, Glass reports that the 2010 and the 2013 CDC *National Intimate Partner and Sexual Violence Survey* confirms that lesbians were more often victimized than heterosexual women.

The science is in. Women in relationships are more violent than men. So why are men always painted as the abusive ones?

Well that answer's easy. Feminist ideologues, in their war on men, mass marketed this lie to society and everyone bought it. Even more impressive, feminists created a corporate welfare driven cottage industry for themselves that simultaneously provided a paycheck and discriminated against men through the creation of the Duluth Model of domestic violence intervention.

In 1983, the Hamline Law Review, published an article by feminist ideologue, Ellen Pence. It revealed to the world her misandric crusade to demonize men, in her article, *"The Duluth Domestic Abuse Intervention Project."*

Pence, a feminist college graduate with an arts degree, got awarded a large grant to create a program to address what she perceived as a problem in domestic violence intervention. Her views, shared by many feminist ideologues of the time, were that not enough men were arrested and convicted of domestic violence.

At the time, domestic violence cases were often dismissed and even when they weren't, the conviction rates were relatively low. The idea that these men might actually be innocent of the crimes they were accused of never entered the conversation. Those accused were men, therefore, they must be guilty. This is supported by Pence's own statements that she believed these outcomes were the result of sexist apologetics and not real justice...in other words...the mythical patriarchy.

To support her bigoted confirmation bias, Pence's next issue is:

> *"the nature of the relationship between the assailant and victim..."*

This fits in nicely with the feminist war on marriage, especially since, at the time, most criminal domestic violence reports were made by women. Why is this an issue? Because if a woman wrongfully accuses her husband of domestic violence, she's more likely to drop the charges later. Which leads us to Pence's next issue,

> *"Traditional responses to domestic assault cases have placed a great deal of responsibility on the victim to participate in evoking and monitoring legal controls on the assailant. Consequently, these responses have often been ineffective. However, intervention which shifts the responsibility of placing controls on the assailant onto community agencies increases the ability of the system to hold assailants responsible for their use of violence."*

In response, Pence's goal was to shift the responsibility away from the woman making the DV report to pretty much anyone else. In 1980, the Domestic Violence

Intervention Project (DAIP) was born.

To move forward, Pence's first order of business was to change the way law enforcement, prosecutors, and the courts perceived domestic violence. She wanted them to stop considering it exclusively as a crime. Pence preferred to look at it as a social problem to support the feminist theory of sexism. To accomplish this, she reframed the crime of domestic violence, not as a crime, but, as a syndrome. Her reasoning in her words is,

> *"The advantage of discussing battering as a syndrome is that it gives us an identifiable group of people with which to work."*

In other words, changing the conversation about domestic violence from criminal/victim paradigm to a syndrome paradigm gave her the pretense she needed to target men.

The DAIP was created as an inter-agency project that consisted of the police department, the county jail, the city attorney's office, the probation department, a women's shelter and four counseling agencies, the Human Development Center, Family Service of Duluth, Lutheran Social Service, and the Duluth Community Health Center. It was overseen by a private non-profit corporation funded by several private sources called the Minnesota Program Development Inc. This non-profit was to coordinate these agencies for a three-year period through three paid employees who were considered DAIP staff.

In 1982, Minnesota's arrest laws changed in favor of Pence's ideology. In Pence's words,

> *"Unlike other misdemeanor offenses, an officer can make an arrest without actually*

> *observing the criminal conduct. The law allows officers to make a probable cause, non-witness arrest on domestic assault calls involving cohabiting adults if the arrest is made within four hours after the alleged assault and there are visible signs of injury or physical impairment to the victim."*

Under Minnesota's laws, even if the woman injures herself or gets injured by something other than domestic violence, she can lie about it and the man gets arrested. Further, if the woman attacks the man with a knife and he fights her off and bruises her, he still gets arrested for domestic violence. That he might actually be the victim is never considered.

What was the police response to DAIP staff telling them to increase the number of arrests? Pence admits she received a lot of resistance from police officers who voiced concerns that this could lead to mandatory arrests, which could create unnecessary legal liability against the police. These sentiments were later echoed by the city attorney's office.

Further, according to Pence, the other most frequent issue police raised, in Pence's words,

> *"the ethics of the policy."*

While no one knew at the time, these cops were completely right to be concerned. Experts would later prove...over and over again...the DAIP was ineffective as a DV intervention tool. Further, they would also prove that using it created an untenable ethical controversy.

When the mandatory arrest policy was fully implemented, it was resisted by the officers on ethical grounds. In response, Pence states,

> "*Several measures were then taken to reach full compliance. First, arresting officers were given written follow-up reports by DAIP staff on the disposition of all cases. Second, dispatcher records on all domestic related calls were reviewed by the inspector of the patrol division to determine whether arrests or investigation reports should have been made. For a two-month period, follow-up phone interviews with all complainants were conducted to determine whether probable cause existed. This somewhat time consuming monitoring resulted in an increase in arrests and will be repeated whenever arrest rates drop over an extended period of time.*"

Think about that for a moment. Every time an officer responded to a DV call, a DAIP feminist ideologue was writing a follow-up report criticizing their response. Further, the officers received more pressure from the inspector of their patrol division, in the form of an ongoing review of each one of their DV calls, and finally, the DAIP feminist ideologues were independently contacting the women complaining of DV to try to get them to file charges.

Remember, DAIP staff weren't trained police officers or forensic investigators. They were untrained man-hating ideologues, led by misandric feminist Ellen Pence who had an undergraduate arts degree.

This was a witch hunt.

Once the police department was brought to heel, the witch hunt shifted focus. They assigned one of the paid feminist DAIP staff to work with each victim, to persuade DV accusers to move forward with prosecution and to prepare the accuser for court. Further, DAIP staff were running their own independent parallel investigations. In Pence's words, their goal was,

> *"to provide the prosecuting attorney with information concerning the case and assistance in evidence gathering, and to assist the prosecutor in making decisions regarding the case (i.e., providing factual information to determine whether a subpoena should be issued and giving sentencing recommendations)."*

Now let's stop and think about that for a moment, DAIP DV advocates were intimately involved in the prosecutor's decision-making process whether to take a case to trial. Additionally, they inserted themselves into a criminal investigation and were also giving sentencing recommendations. These were NOT PROFESSIONALS...they were feminist ideologues. They had no legal training. They weren't attorneys or paralegals. They had no law enforcement or prosecutorial background.

They were feminist ideologues out to persecute men.

Further, to secure more convictions against men, the DAIP staff decided to make the responding police officer, rather than the DV accuser the complaining witness. Knowing that police officers were being substituted as the accuser intimidated many men into falsely pleading guilty.

Finally, in Pence's words,

> *"Finally, the previous practice of dropping charges against the assailant upon the victim's request in writing was eliminated. Instead, the initial interview with the victim*

> *by the prosecutor and the advocate focused on the role of the victim as merely a witness in the case."*

Now I have to stop here.

There are so many things wrong with the DAIP I have to share them. Just like we did before when discussing men falsely accused of rape, those accused of the crime of domestic violence have legal rights granted by common law, court precedent, and the United States Constitution. Anyone accused of a crime in the United States has a right to confront their accuser. They have a right to an impartial jury trial of their peers. They have a right to due process, and they have a right to be considered innocent until proven guilty. While these aren't all the rights the accused have, they're the relevant ones for this conversation.

The DAIP violates all of them.

For example, witness tampering is not only unethical, it's a crime in every state in the United States. In federal cases, it becomes a federal crime. Black's Law Dictionary defines witness tampering, in part, as,

> *"Obstructing justice by harassment, intimidation of the witness before and after testimony."*

When DAIP staff insert themselves into a police investigation, they're potentially tampering with the witness by attempting to persuade them to proceed with criminal prosecution. Further, because they're running their own parallel investigation, they potentially contaminate the chain of evidence and can irreparably taint the investigation.

Given that these DAIP staff don't have any legal

training, for them to be recommending sentencing and assisting in the legal decision-making process of the prosecutor's office, subjects that office to civil liability and accusations of prosecutorial misconduct. This is because of potential wrongful influence from legally-ignorant feminist ideologues.

Even if they did have legal training, they're still bigots, so their involvement in the legal process is of questionable ethics.

In real terms, by virtue of allowing a DV advocate or DAIP staff member to be intimately involved, may be committing the crime of witness tampering to get a man's conviction. DAIP involvement violates a man's due process rights because he cannot be assured a fair and impartial prosecution.

More importantly, because prosecutors are substituting a police officer for the DV accuser, they directly violate the man's right to confront his accuser. This is another example showing that the DAIP could be complicit in denying a man his right to due process under the law. Everyone accused of a crime has a right to confront his accuser.

Like I said before, the DAIP is nothing less than a witch hunt.

In real terms, what does this mean?

In 2008, Adam Liptak reported in the New York Times about attorney Leslie P. Smith, a Virginia lawyer who saw prosecutors coaching and tampering with a witness and then concealed it from defense attorneys. As a result, the target of the tampering, Daryl R. Atkins was convicted of a crime and sentenced to death. Smith repeatedly contacted the State Bar Association for permission to tell the truth. They told him to remain silent or he might lose his ability to practice law. Then, in a stunning reversal, the Bar changed its mind, almost 10 years later. Smith testified in court and Atkins' life was spared because the judge had found the prosecutors guilty of misconduct because they tampered with a witness.

Had Smith not continued to advocate for justice, a man would've died as a direct result of witness tampering by criminal prosecutors.

Even more disturbing, generally speaking, to impartially prove someone is guilty of a crime, it's necessary to prove a clear and unbroken chain of evidence between the crime and the one accused. If untrained laymen, in this case ideological DAIP staff or victim advocates, are conducting their own parallel investigation, inserting themselves into a criminal investigation, or have independent contact with the DV accuser, they potentially break the chain of evidence. If discovered and successfully challenged, a person actually guilty of DV may go free. However, if left undiscovered and unchallenged, an innocent man may be wrongfully convicted and imprisoned.

The following examples show that evidence tampering is more common than people think.

In February 2014, the Christian Science Monitor reported about an evidence tampering case in a Florida crime lab. They report,

> *"Thousands of drug cases handled by a single chemist at a state-run crime lab are under review amid allegations that the chemist might have tampered with drug evidence...The chemist, who works at the*

> *Pensacola Regional Crime Lab, is suspected of removing "large" quantities of prescription pills from evidence packages and replacing them with over-the-counter medications...The allegations of evidence tampering could jeopardize convictions in hundreds of some 2,600 drug cases"*

The following month, in March 2014 in Anchorage, Alaska, KTVA News reports,

> *"A former state crime lab employee is facing six felony charges. Stephen Palmer, 53, is accused of stealing drugs and tampering with evidence."*

Finally, let's look at the case of Annie Dookhan. She's the crime lab chemist, that according to Pro Publica's April 19, 2017, news story,

> *"...has admitted to making up drug test results and tampering with samples, in the process helping send scores of people to prison. Her work may have touched some 24,000 cases."*

That's right...she tainted lab evidence that may have wrongfully convicted and imprisoned to up 24,000 innocent people. Dookhan was eventually convicted and imprisoned for falsifying evidence.

With that in mind, imagine how much damage a man-hating ideologue can do to a criminal prosecution.

Today, the DAIP is better known as the Duluth Model.

This discriminatory feminist witch-hunting program has been implemented throughout the United States, the United Kingdom, Australia, and Parts of Europe. It's been translated into over 22 languages and is the most commonly used DV intervention program in the world.

It's also one of the one of the longest-term recipients of corporate welfare in the history of the United States. It receives not only federal grant monies, but many states have enacted laws requiring its training and use. These mandates created a government funded near monopoly that allows the DAIP to receive stacks of money from conducting required trainings and classes, while simultaneously systemically discriminating against men on a near global scale.

It's a man-hating feminist's dream.

Now I know that I'm sounding a bit evangelical. However, you'll soon see my concerns are reasonably justified.

In March 2006, the peer-reviewed Journal of Aggression and Violent behavior accepted Donald G. Dutton's and Kenneth Corvo's co-authored paper: *"Transforming a Flawed Policy: A Call to Review Psychology and Science In Domestic Violence Research and Practice."*

This paper constituted a meta-study.

Dr. Donald Dutton received his PhD in Social Psychology from the University of Toronto in 1970. He's been involved in researching domestic violence since 1974, even authoring a government report to address it. He was a court approved therapist specializing in DV perpetrators from 1979 to 1985. Dr. Dutton used this experience to develop a psychological model to treat DV abuse. He's an author of 10 books, including three on Domestic Violence, and has published over 122 peer-reviewed articles. As a result of his deep knowledge and experience, he's been called as an expert witness in domestic violence cases, including the high profile O.J. Simpson trial.

Dr. Dutton is a tenured professor in Psychology at the University of British Columbia.

While I know this might seem a bit obvious, I think it's safe to say Dr. Dutton's a little more qualified than Ellen Pence's art degree.

Dr. Ken Corvo received his PhD in Social Welfare in 1993. He has an MSSA in Social Work, an MA in Sociology, and a MS in Urban Studies. He's been a professor at the Syracuse University School of Social Work since 1997 and has taught many courses on family violence, applied research methods and other related material. He's been involved in a number of research and program evaluation projects including: the FHL Foundation, where he wrote and consulted on domestic violence, neuropsychology and attachment theory; Syracuse's Mayor's Commission on Juvenile Violence; The Nord Community Mental Health Center, where he developed, implemented and evaluated an integrated family violence and substance abuse treatment program; The Family Violence Program of Cleveland Ohio, where he developed and implemented an evaluation study of expanded treatment services for perpetrators of domestic violence.

Dr. Corvo is a published author in many peer-reviewed journals and has made many scholarly and academic presentations at conferences across the United States.

It goes without saying that Dr. Corvo's knowledge, training, and experience far surpass Ellen Pence's on her best day.

Right from their opening statement, they debunk the

feminist ideology that is the basis of the Duluth model,

> *"For over thirty years, the public policy response to the problem of domestic violence has been defined by activists as the socially sanctioned dominance of women by men. This view of patriarchy as the sole cause of domestic violence is the underpinning for a policy/practice paradigm that has dominated the regulatory, legal, and policy discourse of the United States, Canada, and other countries. It has influenced legal policy including arrest priorities, prosecutorial decision making, and post arrest intervention. During the same period, researchers from a variety of disciplines have repeatedly found that domestic violence is influenced by a much wider range of factors."*

Dr. Dutton and Dr. Corvo's words are damning and completely debunk the feminist man-hating theory of DV. Even more frightening is that many states have enacted laws to prevent therapeutic intervention in DV. To this end their report states,

> *"In spite of numerous studies identifying...psychological risk features for both genders...many US states and Canadian provinces remain rigidly locked into outmoded and poorly informed policies...any practice that could be construed as psychological treatment is prohibited. Instead these states legislate a variant...called the Duluth Model."*

The primary goal of this model is to get male clients to acknowledge *"male privilege"* and how they have used *"power and control"* to dominate their wives.

Even Dutton and Corvo know this is an ideological witch-hunt used to discriminate against men. More importantly, their research clearly demonstrates that the Duluth model has been almost completely ineffective in reducing or eliminating DV.

In 1999, researchers tested the Duluth model against no DV interventions at all and found no statistically significant differences. While this is just one of many studies they reviewed, they concluded that the outcomes didn't justify mandatory Duluth styled feminist indoctrination.

Even worse for feminists, Dr. Dutton and Dr. Corvo's study completely debunks the feminist theory of patriarchal oppression as the motivator for DV against women. To that end, they state,

> *"Simply put, the evidence for theoretical patriarchy as a "cause" of wife assault is scant and contradicted by numerous studies...women are more likely to use severe violence against non-violent men than the converse."*

Saying the Duluth model is based on junk science and flawed ideologies is being generous. Not only do Dutton and Corvo completely debunk patriarchy as the cause of DV, this debunks the belief that women are oppressed because of patriarchy, in effect, destroying the core ideology of the entire feminist movement.

Feminists lost their mind.

This report not only threatened feminists' entire ideology, it threatened the corporate welfare they were receiving from multiple governments, through grants and fees, to maintain their discriminatory programs.

Millions of man-hating women made their entire careers on the lie that patriarchy oppresses women. This would destroy them. Now even colleges have entire course tracks in man-hating discrimination called "gender studies." One can even get a degree in this debunked ideology.

However, Dutton and Corvo weren't done, they continued down the rabbit hole. In 2009, along with Wan-Yi Chen of Syracuse University, published their paper: "*Do Duluth Model Interventions With Perpetrators of Domestic Violence Violate Mental Health Professional Ethics?*" in the peer-reviewed journal of Ethics and Behavior.

Remember, Ellen Pence previously disclosed that when she first went to develop the Duluth Model, she got pushback from the police because of ethical concerns?

They were right.

Dutton, Corvo, and Chen concluded,

> "*The Duluth Model is clearly at odds with the codes of ethics of the various mental health professions...*
>
> *One may freely chose to undertake therapy, counseling, or some other form of guided change for which there is no evidence of effectiveness. However, the ethical significance of mental health professionals providing compulsory treatment without evidence of effectiveness is another matter.*
>
> *When does treatment become punishment?*
>
> *Moore described court-ordered psychological interventions in general as having the*

> *possibility to become "a punitive wolf in a benevolent sheep's clothing, with the potential for exerting and justifying extensive and harsh punishments*
>
> *In the end this may be as much a matter of private conscience as professional ethics. As mental health professionals, when we enter into a helping relationship with clients, we are asking them to trust us. That trust is founded on a belief that when we bring to bear our professional and socially sanctioned authority, we know what we are doing and that what we do can be reasonably expected to help. Mental Health professionals using the Duluth Model put themselves at risk of violating that trust."*

I can't think of a stronger condemnation of the feminist witch-hunt against men than the words above. Not only did they discover the Duluth model was based on a flawed debunked ideology, it was ineffective and unethical because it targets and punishes men while pretending to help them.

If that isn't the most insidiously evil method to systemically discriminate against a gender, I don't know what is.

While feminists...en masse...demonized and actively attempted to shame Dr. Dutton, Dr. Corvo, and Chen, people were starting to wake up.

In 2009, Johnna Rizza from the University of Montana School of Law penned the article: "*Beyond Duluth: A Broad Spectrum of Treatment for Broad Spectrum of Domestic Violence.*" It was published in the Montana Law Review.

In his research, Rizza confirms the Duluth program,

> "...attempts to halt men's behavior by focusing on the supposed reason they batter...to maintain individual and societal patriarchal dominance. The Duluth Model, does not, however, address other possible reasons for violence, including substance abuse problems, psychological problems, violent backgrounds, or unhealthy relationship dynamics."

He goes even further,

> "Other common risk factors for violence, such as stress on the perpetrator...couples' negative interaction...are systematically excluded as excuses. Any violence perpetrated by a woman is dismissed as either non-existent, self-defensive, or insignificant."

Rizza's paper, while focusing his entire paper on criticism of the Duluth model, confirms Dutton's and Corvo's research and calls for discontinuing its use.

While there are many other scholars and professionals that confirm these findings, all of them have failed to confront the most insidious creation of the Duluth Model. The Family Law Domestic Violence Restraining Order.

The Duluth model created the civil domestic violence order of protection. Feminist ideologue Ellen Pence describes the intent of this new discrimination tool was,

> "...to provide immediate protection without requiring a marriage dissolution action. It was also intended to provide court protection without requiring the victim to initiate a criminal proceeding."

Pence goes on to state that it,

> "...was designed to improve the enforcement of court orders by law enforcement officers and the court by making violation of the order a misdemeanor....to cohabitating adults."

More chilling, is that DAIP feminist ideologues are allowed in the judicial process,

> "Although these is no agreement with family court judges on sentencing for violations of court orders, the DAIP staff makes recommendations when a respondent is found in contempt..."

This type of court action is not criminal, it's civil in nature. Similar to two people suing each other over a car accident. There is a plaintiff and a defendant, though in DV or family court they're often referred to as petitioner and respondent. It's a private party action. However, Pence admits that feminist ideologues are allowed to interfere with this private party action and recommend to a civil family law judge sentencing for violations of DAIP restraining orders.

This risks creating ethical violations for judges under their code of ethics and judicial conduct. Judges are barred from having any ex parte or outside contact with anyone related to any case they are adjudicating. Violation of this has gotten judges removed from the bench in the past and has been the basis for overturning their rulings on appeal. Yet, to Pence, these ethical issues are irrelevant to her war on men.

However, that's not even the worst part. The civil domestic violence restraining order process allows feminists the ability to deny a man his constitutional and legal rights. By accusing him of the crime of domestic violence in a civil court, a man is denied his due process rights guaranteed under the law.

This is because it's a civil court proceeding, the man is forced to waive his 5th amendment to right stay silent, because if he doesn't allege facts demonstrating his innocence, he's automatically found guilty. Further, because he's accused of a crime in a civil court setting, he has no right to a court appointed attorney if he cannot afford one, he has no right to an impartial trial by a jury of his peers. There is no criminal or objective investigation into his accuser's allegations, and he has no right to confront his accuser. More importantly, these orders are awarded on an accelerated schedule. So even if the man has an attorney, unlike any other civil or criminal proceeding, there is no mandated court-allocated time for his attorney to conduct an independent inquiry of the accusations in order to exonerate him.

These due process violations create a perfect storm that, in the majority of cases, the man cannot win. The entire process, by design, is created to discriminate against men.

I believe it's illegal and violates the basic constitutional principles our country and legal system are founded upon.

However, almost all family law judges and judicial staff in the Western world are feminists. As man-hating ideologues, they cannot give a man justice..because their feminist ideology prevents it.

A man accused of the crime of domestic violence getting justice in front of a feminist family law judge would be like an inner city black man expecting to be treated fairly at a trial in a rural county where the judge, jury, and all the court staff are racist members of the KKK.

It's not gonna happen.

Today, civil domestic violence restraining orders are used to evict a man from his home, rob him of his assets, deprive him of his parental right to parent his children free from government interference, while wrongfully publicly humiliating him. This leads to job loss, loss of friends, and loss of community support. This eventually leads to complete isolation.

Is it any wonder a man wrongfully persecuted in such a manner commits suicide and often even kills those around him? Men wrongfully victimized by feminist persecution, even if they don't kill themselves, never fully recover. They lose their entire lives and, more importantly, the respect and love of their children.

It destroys the man and everything around him...including his relationship with his children.

Yet, feminists tell us their ideology is about gender equality.

They're complete liars.

7 FEMALE PRIVILEGE

Since the beginning of feminism, feminists have constantly and loudly complained that patriarchy discriminates against them. To hear them tell it, you'd think that men treated them like chattel or slaves. However, as you're about to see, this is just another lie.

The reality is that, in society, women receive a variety of social and cultural privileges that are almost never mentioned in the gender equality debate. In public spaces, such as busses, trains, and other public areas, a man is expected to relinquish his seat for a woman, so she doesn't have to stand up. However, the reverse isn't true. If a woman is sitting, she is never expected to give up her seat for a man. If a man did refuse, society perceives any man guilty of this as rude.

Annie Pfost shows this in her March 26, 2016, article, *"Where Are the Stand Up Men?"* published by Odyssey Online. She can't even get through her first paragraph without trying to shame men. She states,

> *"It's that men still think their place, their comfort and their butt is more important than a woman's."*

The problem here is that Annie doesn't have the self-awareness to realize how gynocentric and misandric her statement is. Nor does she realize that men, being equal to women, shouldn't put women's comfort before their own. This is especially true if they're women not romantically involved with them. To the narcissistic gynocentric women like Annie, may I suggest you show up earlier to make sure you have a seat?

Now that you've got equal rights, it's time to prove you're equally responsible.

The same double standard holds true for holding doors open for women. In fact, it's so socially unacceptable to hold a door open for a man, when women do it, it's sometimes misconstrued as romantic interest. When men do it for other men, they are careful to avoid eye contact so the other man doesn't misconstrue this random act of kindness as romantic interest.

When women travel, whether it's by plane, train, boat, or automobile, they're prioritized for evacuation and rescue. Further, in emergency rescue and evacuation training, paid staff of transportation organizations, such as airlines, ferry services, and passenger train carriers are often trained to prioritize rescuing and evacuating women over men.

It's even worse in the romantic realm. Women not only expect men to pay for them completely, they demand it. In fact, when taking romantic excursions, if men don't pay, society shames them for it.

Take Jordan Gray for example. Jordan's a "male feminist

relationship coach" (*the comedy here writes itself*) who teaches men to cuck and white knight themselves to women. On September 29, 2014, Jordan penned an article for the Good Men Project entitled, "*Three Reasons Why Guys Should Still be Paying For Dates.*"

Note: The Good Cuck Project is run by feminists as a tool to try to co-opt men into feminism as useful idiots.

Jordan's three reasons are as follows: Firstly, women choose to buy makeup and lingerie. Secondly, he still believes the wage gap lie. Finally, he believes that paying for a woman gets a man a better date. In fact, for people who might question Jordan's wisdom, his article preemptively shames them with,

> "*If you don't feel compelled to pay...you should have...not gone on that particular date in the first place.*"

Unfortunately for this mangina supreme and other fedora-tipping cucklords like him, this is the worst advice you can give to a man in 2017. To break this down, let's look at it from a feminist perspective. By paying for the woman, you're telling her you don't think she's your equal. If she was your equal, she would split the bill equally. However, by paying, you're just admitting you're a knuckle-dragging misogynist from a bygone era.

From a non-feminist perspective, this advice is still garbage. Women who expect men to pay for dates, often just use them for free meals. Most of the time these women have zero romantic interest in the man, but dishonestly lead them on anyway. Take Brittny Pierre, she's just one example of many.

On March 25, 2016, Shantell E. Jamison penned, "*For*

Shame: Woman 'Fesses Up to Using Dates for Free Food." Shantell wrote about Brittny, who admitted,

> *"I decided that I couldn't afford to limit myself to guys I actually wanted to date, I just had to go full throttle and just see who was willing to take me out,"*

In fact, Brittny was so proud of using men, she penned her own article on XOJane, "*It Happened to Me: I cruised OKCupid And Craigslist for Dates So I Could Eat.*" She admitted that even though she graduated from college in 2011, she used men for their money.

> *"I decided I would use OkCupid and Craigslist (yes, even scary ol' Craigslist) so I could have dinner three times a week without opening my wallet...*
>
> *I created a profile, being quite honest about myself, mentioning I'm a writer, what kind of movies I like, how I'm kind of obsessed with dancing and tweeting at the same time, and outlining what kind of guys I'm into.*
>
> *Every day I'd get messages from pretty decent dude.*
>
> *To find my victims, I would chitchat with each possible suitor and then hope they'd offer to take me out, which 9 out of 10 times they would. I would pick a restaurant I wanted to try out in the city and then it was on."*

The scary part is that female predators like Brittny aren't that uncommon. The Pick Up Artist (PUA) community and other parts of the red-pill community refer to this common female behavioral phenomena as the "*alpha fucks, beta bucks"* paradigm.

Yet, if men don't pay for dates, they're still shamed for refusing to cucked.

Which leads into our next example of female privilege, a woman's social status. Men earn status based on their personal and professional accomplishments. Generally, a woman gains status by who she's slept with, not by what she's personally or professionally achieved. While I don't hate women, I can't help but notice the startling similarities between this and parasites that feed off of a host to survive.

While many examples of this abound, a good place to demonstrate this double standard is Robyn Denise Moore. Robyn was an Australian dental nurse who married the actor and filmmaker Mel Gibson. Other than having sex with Gibson, Robyn's accomplished nothing else of note in her life. She was just an average woman from an average background who was married to a multimillionaire filmmaker. However, even though she made no financial contribution to her marriage to Gibson, when she abandoned Gibson after over 30 years of marriage, she took half of Gibson's $850 million dollar wealth with her. That's right, she received over $400 million dollars to abandon her marriage. However, this doesn't include everything Gibson bought her or paid for during his 30 years of commitment to her. In the end, when the numbers are tallied, if you include everything Gibson paid for, Moore got a lot more than $400 million dollars.

Our next strong independent woman is Anna Torv. However, she's better known as Anna Murdoch-Mann. She is the ex-wife of Rupert Murdoch. Murdoch is a media mogul worth over $13 billion dollars. He was the chainman and CEO of News Corp for over 30 years and is now its executive chairman. He was also the chairman and CEO of 21st Century Fox, and is currently the Co-Chair of 21st Century Fox and acting CEO of Fox News. Anna Murdoch is known for...marrying Rupert Murdoch. While married, Rupert gave her a seat on the News Corporation board. Further, even though she's authored three books and worked as a journalist for the Daily Telegraph, none of her works were very noteworthy. Her main accomplishment is abandoning her marriage, getting $1.7 billion dollar settlement, and remarrying someone else six months later.

The next example is Juanita Vanoy. You might better know her as Michael Jordan's ex-wife, Juanita Jordan. Jordan is widely regarded as the greatest professional basketball player ever. As of 2017, he's worth over $1.3 billion dollars. Nike, Jordan's largest sponsor, earns close to $3 billion dollars annually from their Jordan branded shoes. Jordan also maintains endorsements from Upper Deck, Hanes, and Gatorade. So what were Juanita's accomplishments? She was an unsuccessful ex-model who got pregnant by Jordan. Once he found out, he married her. When she abandoned their marriage she received a $168 million dollar settlement, which at the time, set the world record for largest celebrity divorce settlement on public record.

Which leads us into the next area of female privilege, parental rights. Few areas demonstrate female privilege as clearly as the subject of parental rights. In the United States, a woman can legally choose to abort, adopt, abandon, or keep her child. The child's father has no say in these decisions. Now, I appreciate the counter-argument that a woman cannot adopt out her child without the father's consent. However, if the mom claims she doesn't know who the father is and conceals the pregnancy from the father, then the adoption can legally move forward. In fact, because of safe-haven laws, if the mom conceals the pregnancy from the father, she can legally abandon her child in many jurisdictions by dropping that child off at a hospital or a fire station.

However, a father doesn't have any of those rights. He has no legal right to determine whether the child should be aborted. In fact, if a father chooses to abandon a child, he's considered a deadbeat dad while the mother is lionized for being "brave."

Usually when this topic comes up, the response I get from feminists is,

> *"Well, they both chose to have sex, so he should be responsible."*

This response demonstrates feminists complete lack of self-awareness. Look at the statement again. "They" chose to have sex. "He" should be responsible. Feminists never advocate for a woman to share responsibility. They only advocate for men to be responsible for the consequences of a woman's decisions, regardless of the negative impact.

There's no stronger example of this than the epidemic of paternity fraud in Western society. Ronald K. Henry penned an article for the Spring 2006 edition of the peer-reviewed Family Law Quarterly, entitled, *"The Innocent Third Party, Victims of Paternity Fraud."*

Henry writes,

> *"Paternity fraud has always been a risk for cuckolded husbands and for wealthy or famous men. As reported in one famous paternity fraud case: The former wife of billionaire Kirk Kerkorian has admitted the four-year-old girl for whom he is being asked*

> *to pay more than $320,000 in support is not his child and she faked DNA tests."*

However, Henry goes on to state that even though the rich can often be subjected to paternity fraud, with the rise of non-marital births,

> *"...the vast bulk of men who are at risk for paternity fraud victimization are neither rich nor famous."*

How prevalent is paternity fraud? Henry states the American Associations of Blood Banks, found that close to 28% of paternity tests conducted in California excluded the man identified as the father, as being the biological father. In California alone, the paternity fraud rate is close to 3 in 10. However, this number doesn't include those instances where the father is clueless and paternity isn't challenged.

This is confirmed by Premier Screenings. Premier Screenings is Florida based company that's a third party administrator and lab testing facility that does DNA testing, lab tests, drug and background checks, and DOT Compliance Services. They're partnered with the largest accredited and CLIA-certified laboratories throughout the United States. Their clients include law enforcement agencies and state counties. Their website states,

> *"About 300,000 DNA tests are conducted to establish paternity every year and 30% of these tests showed that the man is not the biological father of the child."*

There you have it, 3 in 10 unmarried fathers in the United States are cucked and fraudulently held responsible for children that aren't theirs. However, to be fair, this number could be far higher. This only represents fathers who've questioned their paternity.

Sadly, if you're in the UK, this number is a lot higher. According to Lucy Roue's report in the Manchester Evening News, from January 1, 2017, *"Nearly Half of Men Who Take Paternity Test Are Not The Real Father."*

She reports,

> *"Testing firm DNA Clinics, which is part of the Salford-based BioClinics Group, analyzed 5,000 results selected randomly from between January 2014 and June 2016.*
>
> *The results show 48 per cent or 2,396 of UK men tested were not the biological father.*
>
> *For England as a whole, 51 per cent were ruled out as being the paternal father. In Northern Ireland, 42 per cent were ruled out while in Scotland the figure was 39 per cent."*

You guys across the pond are cucked more often than us yankees.

What's the position of feminist organizations and leaders on the subject of women who commit paternity fraud?

They don't have one. Their silence is deafening.

Even more disturbing is the trend of women who choose to steal a man's sperm and fraudulently impregnate themselves to trap a man with a child. It's called sperm jacking. The Urban Dictionary defines sperm jacking as,

> *"the involuntary collection of a man's sperm, generally committed by females who desire to have a child with a male with no*

such desire."

How is this accomplished? A Reddit poster named feminista8 describes one method in her now five-year-old Reddit post on r/ShitRedditSays, reprinted here in its entirety.

Feminista8:

> *"Sedditors contribute valuable sperm, and, if you play your cards right, child support. Here's how it works, ladies:*
>
> *Find your alpha. Go to a bar, or a club, or a concert. Someplace where you can make a bit of small talk, drink, and easily get away with physical harassment contact. Look for a dude who's standing on the sides, swaying to the music. Ask him to dance. If he says no, don't sweat it. Just skip to step 2. Dance for a short while, stop just before he begins to have fun.*
>
> *Buy him a drink. Chat him up. Nothing meaningful, obviously, it can be stuff you don't care about. Like his job, or favorite show, or friends. Then buy him another drink. Don't worry, it's not that you're getting him drunk, you're just...relaxing his boundaries. Dudes totally need to have their boundaries relaxed. Society's just so tough on alphas, you know?*
>
> *COMMENCE KINO. If he says no or pushes your hands away, just wait a bit, buy him another drink, and try again. Remember, "no" means "not just yet".*
>
> *Once you've established kino, mention some*

cool movie you just bought that day. (It doesn't have to be true, in fact, it's probably best to lie whenever talking about yourself so your target doesn't realize what a sad lump of organic waste you are.) Try to make it a James Bond movie, or a Tarantino film. Alphas love Tarantino. Wait for him to mention this.

Invite him over. If he says no, buy him another drink until he says "ye-ghbarlagh"

On the way back to your place, transition from kino to measuring his height, skull, bone density, and any possibly heart conditions. You'll want to establish the value of his semen before you collect it, so you don't waste valuable freezer space.

It's turkey baster time, baby.

Remember to make copies of his drivers license, credit cards, and phone records before he leaves. If he asks questions the next day, creep shame him until he stops. If you decide to use his semen for child support units, be sure to false rape accuse him during custody hearings.

Good luck out there, champ! ;)"

While you might think this is a rare phenomenon, it's not. As you'll find out later, a survey found that women lie about being on birth control, at least, 42% of the time.

On November 3, 2011, Liz Jones wrote her sperm jacking confession in the Daily Mail article, *"The Craving For A Baby That Drives Women to the Ultimate Deception."*

She confesses,

> *"I had hatched a plan that many will doubtless find shocking...Because he wouldn't give me what I wanted, I decided to steal it from him. I resolved to steal his sperm from him in the middle of the night. I thought it was my right, given that he was living with me...*
>
> *One night, after sex, I took the used condom and, in the privacy of the bathroom, I did what I had to do."*

Thankfully, she didn't get pregnant and her victim escaped. However, that didn't stop her. She goes on to admit,

> *"But my dreams of motherhood persisted, and I resorted to similarly secretive methods to conceive in my next relationship."*

Thankfully, Liz was such a loser that she failed her second time as well. After the second failed attempt, she appears to give up. While this is first-hand look into hypergamous women with baby rabies, she inadvertently reports something extremely telling.

It turns out that women do attempt to trap men in unwanted pregnancies far more often than one might think. Jones reports,

> *"A 2001 survey revealed that 42 per cent of women would lie about using contraception in order to get pregnant in spite of their partners' wishes."*

Think about that for a moment. Almost half of all women would lie about using contraception. Yet, when men complain about having unwanted children, feminists shame them for it.

As a man, you might think, *"I won't get her pregnant if I only allow her give me a blow-job."* Think again. On February 4, 2014, Lincoln Anthony Blades reports in Uptown Magazine,

> *"A doctor named Sharon Irons was having an affair with a Chicago family physician named Richard Phillips. Apparently, they never had sexual intercourse, but she would perform oral sex on him. Well, after Phillips ejaculated in Irons' mouth one night, she decided to store the semen in her cheeks and then spit it into a test tube. She later used the semen to impregnate herself."*

Now Dr. Irons' theft was successful and later she filed a successful paternity lawsuit and now Dr. Phillips has to pay over $800 in child support.

Sperm jacking has become so common that women are evolving ever more advanced theft techniques. Shawna Cohen, on November 23, 2011, penned the article, *"Woman Steals Ex-Boyfriend's Sperm, Has Twins, Sues for Child Support."*

The subject of her article, a woman only identified only as Anatria, trapped her ex-boyfriend, Joe Pressil, with an unwanted pregnancy by stealing his sperm in 2007. They'd been broken up for three months when she told him she was pregnant. However, he didn't believe her because they'd always used birth control. Nevertheless, a paternity test confirmed he was the father.

What happened? Cohen tells us,

> *"Fast forward to February of this year*

> *(2011), when 36-year-old Pressil found a receipt – from a Houston sperm bank called Omni-Med Laboratories – for "cryopreservation of a sperm sample" (Pressil was listed as the patient although he had never been there). He called Omni-Med, which passed him along to its affiliated clinic Advanced Fertility. The clinic told Pressil that his "wife" had come into the clinic with his semen and they performed IVF with it, which is how Anetria got pregnant."*

Anatria lied to a sperm bank after stealing Pressil's sperm to have it preserved to get pregnant later.

Remember, 42% of women would lie about using birth control. Yet, if they do, they suffer no consequences for getting pregnant through fraud.

However, that isn't even the worst of it. Imagine being a man sexually assaulted by a woman. Later you find out your rapist got pregnant with your child and the courts order you to pay child support for a child conceived in rape. That's exactly what happened to Nick Olivas.

Nick was raped when he was 13-year-old teenager. His child abuser birthed his child when he was just 14 years old. In 2014, the Arizona child support authority told him he owed about $15,000 to his child rapist for child support.

While these types of cases are rare, Olivas isn't the only male child abuse victim forced to pay child support for a child conceived by their child molester. Olivas' rapist was never charged for her crime.

Speaking of double standards, date rape is a huge plank in the feminist platform. While in principle, this seems a legitimate grievance. However, on closer inspection, the hypocrisy presents itself in feminism's "alcohol induced" date rape campaign.

The theory is that women who have imbibed alcohol are unable to give legitimate consent, therefore feminist organizations have reframed consensual sex with an intoxicated woman as rape.

This view, while common across the feminist ideological sphere, is exemplified by Margaret Wente in her 2014 Globe and Mail article, "Can She Consent to Sex After Drinking?"

She reports,

> *"Can a woman consent to sex when she's been drinking? Universities have decided that the answer is no. ...Although that sentence is crafted to be gender-neutral, its warning is directed at men. It means that drunken sex is tantamount to rape...*
>
> *Is there a double standard here? Indeed there is. Men are treated as potential rapists, and women as their helpless victims...If two young people get hammered and have drunken sex, he is responsible for his behaviour, but she's not responsible for hers."*

This view isn't shared by Wayne MacKay, the law professor who wrote the 110-page rape task force report for Saint Mary's College that Wente's article criticizes. When Wente interviewed MacKay, he stated,

> *"Clearly the focus needs to be on the fact that men need to have a better understanding and stop raping."*

As we saw in an earlier chapter, the consequences of promoting rape culture are often severe. College campuses are throwing due process out the window. Men accused of sexual assault are deemed guilty until proven innocent, and many are expelled.

Wente's piece rightly exposes the hypocrisy of the feminist view of alcohol involved consensual sex reframed as a man raping a woman. However, by the same logic, if a man is intoxicated, then he cannot consent either.

Now, I'm not discussing women who've passed out and the man forces himself on her unconscious body. I'm specifically referring to drunk women who actually consent to sex, then later regret it and falsely claim it's rape. It's like saying a drunk driver who kills someone shouldn't be imprisoned because the alcohol prevented him from being responsible for his actions.

What if she's sober and he's drinking, he consents to sex, does that make the woman a rapist also? What if both are drunk when they consent, are they both rapists?

The whole concept is lunacy. The most hypocritical aspect of these types of rape campaigns is that they're funded and supported by feminist organizations across the world, yet they completely infantilize women by claiming women who've imbibed alcohol cannot consent to sex.

It's like feminists don't want women held accountable or to be responsible for their actions. Few things can be more hypocritically misogynistic.

Speaking of women in crime, have you noticed that when women and men commit the same types of crimes, the man always gets an increased sentence? Sonja Starr noticed this also. She's a law professor and co-director of the Empirical Legal Studies Center at the University of Michigan's Law School. On August 29, 2012, she published a paper entitled, *"Estimating Gender Disparities in Federal Criminal Cases."*

Professor Starr found,

> "...dramatic unexplained gender gaps in federal criminal cases...men receive 63% longer sentences on average than women do. Women are also significantly likelier to avoid charges and convictions, and twice as likely to avoid incarceration if convicted."

Australian legal researchers found a similar pattern. Dr. Samantha Jeffries and Christine E W Bond with the support of the South Australian Office of Crime Statistics and Research, published their 2010 study, *"Sex and Sentencing Disparity in South Australia's Higher Courts,"* in the peer-reviewed journal Current Issues in Criminal Justice.

Their study found,

> "Consistent with official criminal justice data, women's offending behaviours tended to be less serious than men's, but even when these factors were controlled, women were sentenced more leniently than men. A direct relationship between sex and sentencing was found: when women and men appeared before South Australia's higher courts for comparable criminality (past and present), women were less likely to be imprisoned and, when sentenced to prison received shorter terms"

Clearly, there's no feminist outcry at the gender

inequality of the criminal justice system. It's just one more example of female privilege.

Finally, let's look at the U.S. military draft. If you're an adult male in the United States, at 18 years old, you have to register for military selective service. If you don't, you cannot vote, you cannot receive financial aid for college, nor can you get employment with a federal agency.

However, at the time of this writing, women don't have to register for selective service, but get all those privileges anyway.

The next time a feminist tries to tell you how oppressed women are, you'll know they're lying.

8 FEMINISM HARMS WOMEN

Two of the primary enemies of feminism are the institution of marriage and family values. By all objective measurements, feminists have succeeded in defeating both. In earlier chapters, we've seen the devastation feminists have forced onto men and communities in general, through witch-hunting and gender discrimination. However, we've not really discussed feminism's impact on women.

It's been a long road, but women have started to realize, especially with feminism, actions have consequences.

When feminists started attacking marriage they knew they needed a carrot to entice women away from their comfortable and healthy family lives. Their solution was to promote the instant gratification related benefits of being promiscuous. However, historically, being promiscuous was not without major consequences, namely pregnancy. In order to mitigate promiscuity's impact on women, feminists rallied behind both birth control and abortion.

Simply put, feminists enticed women to have as much sex as they could with the promise to avoid the natural consequences through a combination of birth control and abortion. Once their plan was contrived, they reframed being a slut as a gendered issue and the sexual liberation movement was born.

However, being short-sighted, feminists never considered the long-term societal consequences of destroying the institution of marriage and family values through promiscuity.

Rampant promiscuity had a major impact on communities by increasing the need for a welfare state and was a major contributor to communities racked by epidemic crime and uncontrollable drug addiction. On the home front, the "sexual liberation" movement destroyed not just marriages...but entire families.

What are the specifics of these natural consequences?

Well first, let's discuss birth control. While it prevents unwanted pregnancies, what are some of the other ramifications?

Birth control pills are so common today that they're being prescribing for purposes other than pregnancy prevention. Today, doctors are prescribing them for acne prevention, irregular periods, and even PMS. Even though birth control pills are generally safe, there are side-effects to taking them that can have potentially fatal long-term consequences.

One of the main issues with birth control is that it causes weight gain. Whenever this is brought up, it's minimized. Further, even the professionals deny this is an issue. Why are we talking about it? It's because the studies mainly measure solid-mass gain, not bloating.

Zahra Barnes from Self Magazine interviewed OB/GYN Dr. Idries Abdur-Rahman for her Self Magazine article, *"The Truth About Birth Control Causing Weight Gain"* published August 13, 2016. Dr. Abdur-Rahman states,

> *"The short answer is...it can."*

Dr. Alyssa Dweek, professor from Mount Sinai School of Medicine told Barnes,

> *"you shouldn't experience significant weight gain..."*

On January 2, 2014, the meta-study, *"Effect of Birth Control Pills and Patches on Weight,"* published in the Cochrane Database of Systematic Reviews, states,

> *"Most studies of different birth control methods showed no large weight difference.*
>
> *The evidence was not strong enough to be sure that these methods did not cause some weight change."*

It's clear the researchers did find some weight gain. They go on to state that after reviewing these trials,

> *"Available evidence was insufficient to determine the effect of combination contraceptives on weight..."*

Woman's Health journalist Alexandria Gomez published her article *"Is Your Birth Control REALLY Making You Gain Weight"* on April 27, 2017. Gomez interviewed Dr. Mary Jane Minkin, professor at the Yale University School of Medicine and reports,

> *"Weight gain is common complaint...for many patients. The problem is that, for the most part, the reason why hormonal birth control might make you gain weight is a mystery."*

Dr. Minkin confirms the experts have no idea why hormonal birth control causes weight gain. However, at the same time, it's clear that it does. What's sad is that even though everyone knows birth control causes weight gain, everyone, goes out of their way to minimize discussion about it.

Even more concerning is how birth control is linked to mental health issues.

Dr. Jayashri Kulkarni is a professor of psychiatry at the Alfred and Monash University in Melbourne Australia. Not only is she a professor, but she also directs the Monash Alfred Psychiatry Research Centre. It's a large psychiatric research group of over 100 professionals from a variety of fields.

Dr. Kulkarni published a study entitled, *"Depression as a side effect of the contraceptive pill,"* in the July 2006 edition of the peer-reviewed journal, Expert Opinion on Drug Safety. She found,

> *"Millions of women worldwide use the combined oral contraceptive pill as an effective form of contraception. However, the focus on its side effects to date has mainly been on physical aspects, even though the most commonly stated reason for discontinuation is depression. There are surprisingly few large studies investigating depression related to oral contraceptive use. A pilot study was conducted showing that women using the combined oral*

> *contraceptive pill were significantly more depressed than a matched group who were not."*

Even in 2007, there was objective evidence that birth control was linked to depression.

Fast forward to November 2016. The peer-reviewed Journal of the American Medical Association, JAMA Psychiatry, published, *"Association of Hormonal Contraception With Depression."* It was a study conducted by Charlotte Wessel Skovlund MSc, Dr. Lina Steinrud Morch, and Dr. Lars Vedel Kessing.

What it found was damning,

> *"Millions of women worldwide use hormonal contraception. Despite the clinical evidence of an influence of hormonal contraception on some women's mood, associations between the use of hormonal contraception and mood disturbances remain inadequately addressed.*
>
> *In a nationwide...study of more than 1 million women...an increased risk for first use of an antidepressant and first diagnosis of depression was found among users of different types of hormonal contraception, with the highest rates among adolescents.*
>
> *Use of hormonal contraception, especially among adolescents, was associated with subsequent use of antidepressants and a first diagnosis of depression, suggesting depression as a potential adverse effect of hormonal contraceptive use."*

The science is clear. Hormonal birth control is definitely

linked to mental health problems. However, that's not the end of it. It turns out that taking birth control can also increase a woman's chances of getting breast cancer. The Susan Komen Foundation, in its list of factors that can increase the chance of breast cancer states,

> *"Current or recent use of birth control pills (oral contraceptives) slightly increases the risk of breast cancer. Studies show while women are taking birth control pills (and shortly after), they have a 20-30 percent higher risk of breast cancer than women who have never used the pill."*

While feminists are pushing women to get on birth control, it turns out the costs might not be worth the benefit after all. However, feminists constantly minimize and dismiss these facts, because it destroys their narrative.

What about abortion? Are there downsides here also?

In the United States, for a long time, almost all medical professionals have agreed that abortion isn't associated with increased cancer risk. However, outside the United States, it's a far different story.

The February 2014 edition of Cancer Causes & Control, an international peer-reviewed journal of studies of cancer in human populations, published, *"A Meta-Analysis of the Association Between Induced Abortion and Breast Cancer Among Chinese Females."*

This meta-study was co-authored by 13 professionals from the following nationally recognized organizations:

1. Chinese Department of Epidemiology and Biostatisticsm located at the Tainjin Medical University Cancer Hospital and Institute and National Research

Center for Cancer

2. The Chinese Key Laboratory of Cancer Prevention and Therapy in Tainjin, China

3. The Chinese Key Laboratory of Breast Cancer Prevention and Therapy, Tainjin Medical University, Ministry of Education.

4. The Department of Social Medicines and Health Service Management, School of Public Health located at the Tainjin Medical University.

5. The Tainjin Women's and Children's Health Center Project Office.

As you can see, this wasn't a study conducted by some crackpot in their backyard. This was a study conducted by Chinese professionals from some of the most prestigious institutions in China. What they found was also deeply disturbing. Their conclusion was,

> *"I.A. (induced abortion) is significantly associated with an increased risk of breast cancer among Chinese females, and the risk of breast cancer increases as the number of IA increases."*

So according to over a dozen professionals from the some of the most prestigious cancer treatment and research centers in China, the more abortions a woman has...the greater the risk of breast cancer.

Further, the following year, on April 7, 2015, the American College of Pediatricians (ACPeds) issued a press release, "Know Your ABCs: The Abortion Breast Cancer Link," stating,

> *"The American College of Pediatricians*

> *urges women to "Know your ABCs" since abortion appears to be linked to breast cancer. Although the medical community has been reluctant to acknowledge the link, induced abortion prior to a full term delivery, and prior to 32 weeks of gestation, increases the likelihood that a woman will develop breast cancer. This risk is especially increased for adolescents."*

The ACPeds' press release later cites a study conducted by cancer specialist Dr. Rebecca Johnson from Seattle Children's hospital. She found,

> *"Evidence suggests that IA (induced abortion) prior to a full-term pregnancy contributes to the high rates of breast cancer seen around the world. The current studies demonstrating a dose-related association between pre-term induced abortion and breast cancer strongly suggest a causal effect.*
>
> *Although further study is warranted, this risk must be known by adolescent females. The American College of Pediatricians recommends that all medical professionals provide this information as part of complete health care to all adolescents and their parents. It is important that parents reinforce this information to their daughters.*
>
> *All health educators should include this information in any health/sexuality education class in which abortion is discussed."*

The abortion cancer link is also confirmed in the UK by Patrick S. Carroll, Jean S. Utshudiema, and Julian

Rodrigues in their article, "*The British Breast Cancer Epidemic: Trends, Patterns, Risk Factors, and Forecasting,*" published in Journal of American Physicians and Surgeons, Spring 2017. They found,

> "*The reproductive and hormonal risk factors known to affect breast cancer include...induced abortion...Although still contested, there is significant literature that demonstrates that induced abortion...raise the risk of developing breast cancer.*"

This is cannot be any more damning.

When I say that feminist-inspired promiscuity is destroying women's lives, I'm not just being hyperbolic. As promiscuity increases, inevitably, so does the use of birth control and potentially abortion, sometimes both. They both also increase cancer risk in women.

Not only does promiscuity lead to higher cancer risk, it also damages women in other ways.

Dr. Chris Iliades' June 15, 2010, peer-reviewed article in Everyday Health, "*Is There A Price to Pay for Promiscuity?*" demonstrates that promiscuity threatens long-term health. He says,

> "*The more sexual partners you have, the greater your risk for sexually transmitted diseases (STDs) like HIV/AIDS and other life-threatening conditions like prostate cancer, cervical cancer, and oral cancer.*"

Quoting Dr. Deidre Lee Fitzgerald, professor of psychology from Eastern Connecticut State University in Walliamantic, Dr. Iliades goes on to state,

> "*Promiscuity is one example of a class of*

> *high-risk behaviors...It is comparable to, and may coincide with, behaviors such as heavy drinking, gambling, and other thrill-seeking behaviors like driving too fast."*

However, this was known almost 20 years earlier, when in September 1992, the University of Michigan's School of Public Health's Department of Epidemiology published the study, *"Multiple Partners and Partner Choice as Risk Factors for Sexually Transmitted Disease Among Female College Students."*

That study found,

> *"Multiple sexual partners and partner choice are believed to increase the risk if sexually transmitted disease (STD), but these behaviors had not previously been assessed outside of clinical populations.*
>
> *There was a strong association between the number of sexual partners and having an STD: those women with 5 or more sexual partners were 8 times more likely to report having an STD than those with only 1 partner, even after adjusting for age at first intercourse...*
>
> *The prevalence of a history of STDs increased with more causal partner choice and earlier age at first intercourse"*

However, by their mid 20s, we all know that many women now have far more than five sexual partners. For many women, five sexual partners is low. Based on STD numbers, it seems that promiscuity is on the rise in the United States. The United States Center for Disease Control (CDC) issued a press release on November 17, 2015,

> "Reported cases of three nationally notifiable STDs – chlamydia, gonorrhea, and syphilis – have increased for the first time since 2006...STDs continue to affect young people – particularly women--most severely...contributed to the overall increases in 2014 across all three diseases.
>
> "America's worsening STD epidemic is a clear call for better diagnosis, treatment, and prevention," said Jonathan Mermin, M.D., director of CDC's National Center for HIV/AIDS, Viral Hepatitis, STD, and Tuberculosis Prevention. "STDs affect people in all walks of life, particularly young women...
>
> The 2014 data also show that youth are still at the highest risk of acquiring an STD, especially chlamydia and gonorrhea. Despite being a relatively small portion of the sexually active population, young people between the ages of 15 and 24 accounted for the highest rates of chlamydia and gonorrhea in 2014 and almost two thirds of all reported cases. Additionally, previous estimates suggest that young people in this age group acquire half of the estimated 20 million new STDs diagnosed each year.
>
> Despite recommendations from the CDC and the United States Preventive Services Task Force (USPSTF) for annual chlamydia and gonorrhea screening for sexually active women younger than 25, experts believe far too many young people are not tested, and therefore don't know they are infected."

Now with increased medical technology and the fact

that all three of these diseases are curable, why is the CDC so concerned about the increasing STD rate in the United States? It's because they know that as more people get STDs, they greater their chances of getting HIV.

The CDC stated,

> *"In the United States, people who get syphilis, gonorrhea, and herpes often also have HIV or are more likely to get HIV in the future. One reason is the behaviors that put someone at risk for one infection (...multiple partners, anonymous partners) often put them at risk for other infections.*
>
> *Also, because STD and HIV tend to be linked, when someone gets an STD it suggests they got it from someone who may be at risk for other STD and HIV. Finally, a sore or inflammation from an STD may allow infection with HIV that would have been stopped by intact skin."*

The CDC's message is very clear, the more sexual partners a person has, the greater the risk of STDs, and more importantly, the greater the risk of contracting HIV. Also, don't forget, both the CDC and University of Michigan said that women are especially vulnerable populations.

Why is that?

Paul Sims answers the question in his December 9, 2008, article in the Daily Mail, *"In the Age of Promiscuity, Women Have More Sexual Partners Than Men."* He reports that women are now far more promiscuous than men. His reporting focused on a survey conducted by More Magazine that found,

> *"Young women are becoming more promiscuous, with more sexual partners than men, researchers have found.*
>
> *By the age of 21 they have had sex with an average of nine lovers...And a quarter have slept with more than ten partners in the five years since losing their virginity - compared with a fifth of young men.*
>
> *Young women are also twice as likely to be unfaithful, with 50 per cent admitting they have cheated on a partner - half at least twice*
>
> *The survey found more than half of the women were not in love with the person to whom they lost their virginity.*
>
> *Seven out of ten confessed to having had a one-night stand and a fifth had enjoyed more than five.*
>
> *One in four said they would marry for money whilst 39 per cent would sleep with their boss for a promotion. And 27 per cent would have an affair with a married man, while 14 per cent would sleep with their best friend's partner."*

Clearly, feminism's sexual liberation movement bears a lot of responsibility here. As feminist women's promiscuity increased, so did their likelihood of contracting sexually transmitted diseases, HIV, and cancer.

However, it doesn't end there. Being promiscuous has mental health consequences as well. Dr. Susan Kraus Whitbourne talks about them in her two articles for

Psychology Today. Her first, published on March 9, 2013, "*How Casual Sex Can Affect Our Mental Health*" reports,

> "*In a comprehensive review of the status of research on casual sex, Kinsey Institute researcher Justin Garcia and his team from Binghamton University (2012) concluded that "Hookups are part of a popular cultural shift that has infiltrated the lives of emerging adults throughout the Westernized world.*
>
> *...hookups pose a significant threat to the...psychological health...*
>
> *people who engage in casual sex may suffer emotional consequences that persist long after the details of an encounter are a dim memory.*
>
> *Researchers examining the mental health associations of hookup sex also report that participants who were not depressed before showed more depressive symptoms and loneliness after engaging in casual sex.*
>
> *people who engaged in more hookups had greater psychological distress.*"

In Dr. Kraus Whitbourne's second Psychology Today article, published the following month, on April 20, 2013, "*The Lingering Psychological Effects of Multiple Sex Partners,*" she reports that,

> "*For both men and women, taking into account prior psychological disorders, the odds of developing substance dependence increased virtually linearly with the number*

> *of sex partners. The relationship was particularly pronounced, however, for women.*
>
> *The authors acknowledge that, even though they ruled out the effects of prior substance use on number of sex partners, the possibility remains that people living a risky lifestyle have a higher number of sex partners and, later on, develop mental health problems."*

The greater the number of sexual partners, the greater the likelihood of developing drug addictions and mental health problems. What does that mean for relationships?

DARA, the Drug and Alcohol Rehab center, on their website alcoholrehab.com doesn't mince words with their answer. They state,

> *"Alcohol and drug abuse is the source of many problems...One of the earliest casualties from substance abuse will be intimacy. It is just not possible for people to abuse mind altering substances and maintain healthy relationships.*
>
> *As the individual falls deeper into addiction it will completely take over their life, and there will be no room for anyone else.*
>
> *The person falls into delusion and self absorption, and they will stay that way until they manage to escape their addiction. Once they enter recovery they will need to work hard in order to regain the ability to be intimate and enjoy healthy sexual relationships."*

However, to take it a step further, Beth Watson, LCSW authored a blog post from August 21, 2013, *"Promiscuity A Form of Self-Mutilation?"* She states that promiscuity has become a form of self-mutilation in fatherless girls. In citing other professionals, Watson states,

> *"For girls who grow up without fathers, it's not unusual to act out sexually and look for validation in all the wrong places.*
>
> *Promiscuity is often observed as a common practice among "daddyless daughters" and is just one possible effect of not having a father figure. It's also something Dr. Steve Perry, founder of Capital Preparatory Magnet School, has seen in his work with fatherless girls, leading him to a startling definition of promiscuity as a whole.*
>
> *"Promiscuity is the main thing," Dr. Perry says in "It's rarely seen as self-mutilation, but that's exactly what it is."*
>
> *Dr. Perry continues, "Often when we look at young girls who are dealing with pain, we think of self-mutilation as the cutting. That too, but promiscuity is the self-mutilation of allowing someone to physically enter you."*

Young women using sex as a form of self-mutilation is another consequence of promiscuity culture.

Simply put, feminists harmed women by selling them a lie.

Feminism used the sexual liberation movement to destroy the institution of marriage and family values. In doing so, it created a promiscuity culture that, according to the CDC, created and worsened the United States STD epidemic. Just as troubling, it's also directly associated with increased mental problems in women through a combination of the act of casual sex itself and the use of birth control.

Additionally, it's been found that the more sexual partners one has, the greater the likelihood of drug addiction. Further, promiscuity, through the use of birth control and abortions, increased women's cancer risks dramatically. In the end, feminism's promotion of promiscuity culture created a spiraling problem that leads to daughters from fatherless homes using casual sex as a form of self-mutilation, making the problem worse.

While feminists try to deny their involvement in creating the promiscuity culture, one only needs to look to the feminist organized and funded slut walks to debunk this lie. Regardless of how feminists lie, the reality is that promiscuity has far-reaching and long-term consequences

9 FEMINISM'S REACTION

Feminists learned early on that their voices alone weren't enough to further feminism. Their solution was to establish a network of male allies and co-opt other movements to silence critics and spread their beliefs. These male allies are known by feminists as male feminists. However, rationally minded people rightfully refer to them as either: manginas, white knights, pussy-beggars, or cucks.

Why is this? It's because male feminists don't function as allies. They function as servants and useful idiots to the feminist movement. They're often motivated by their desire to set themselves apart from men that feminists attack to gain sexual access to these women.

Their reward, more often than not, is to be permanently exiled to the friendzone. However, there are male feminists who actually do form relationships with feminists. Some are even able to marry them. When this happens, it's normally because the mangina in question has an extremely well-paying job, high social status, or both. However, behind closed doors, their wives cuckold them through infidelity or more openly, by letting them know they're not committed to their mangina husbands by asking for open relationships.

However, male feminist cucks are so indoctrinated they fail to see the brutal irony and self-destructiveness of their situation. Meanwhile, their feminist masters laugh about it behind their backs.

One example of the male feminist recruitment program is the *"He for She"* movement. It was a global propaganda campaign founded by the United Nations Entity for Gender Equality and the Empowerment of Women. Even the name of the campaign demonstrates its mission to get men to subordinately serve women's interests.

Why not call it cucks for chicks?

The face of the movement? Actress Emma Watson, an extremely rich, self-made woman, who claims women aren't equal and need all the help they can get. Her own achievements clearly show the hypocrisy and dishonesty of her words. If she can be a successful millionaire, so can anyone else, with the right investment of time and effort.

This campaign has critics within feminism and without. Within feminism, other subsets are jealous of it because it doesn't focus more on insane non-binary individuals and people suffering from transgender delusions. Further, even normal feminists have said the movement's name is misogynist because it claims women need men. While the movement has received criticism from both sides of the issue, feminists and anti-feminists both agree the campaign itself is hypocritical.

Sadly, tradcon men have become just as bad. They're so naively misogynistic they don't see feminists as equals, but rather as special snowflakes to be protected...until they're divorce raped. In conservative states, it's tradcons who've voiced their opposition to feminism that end up passing most feminist inspired domestic violence and rape laws that discriminate against men.

Few things can be more idiotic and against self-interest.

If you laugh about divorce rape and think it can't happen to you, think again. In earlier chapters, I provided some examples of highly successful alpha males whose wives left them and stole millions of dollars on the way out. If your response is, "well, they didn't have that high of a sexual market value." You're still being naive. Johnny Depp and Brad Pitt were both considered the sexiest men alive. Women across the globe openly offered to commit to them and sire their children. Both eventually married. Both were falsely accused of domestic abuse and got divorced raped by their wives, women who were both feminists. However, when Brad Pitt and Angelina Jolie married, she was a conservative.

The takeaway: married feminists almost always try to divorce rape their husbands. It's not a question of if, it's a question of when.

With feminists useful cucks in place, what's feminism's response been to legitimate criticism?

First, it's usually to shame the critic with personal attacks or reframe the argument without ever addressing any of the critic's issues. In the case of Everyday Feminism's author Shannon Ridgway, who penned an article entitled, "*25 Everyday Examples of Rape Culture*," it's to spread the lie that rape culture is real.

Even though RAINN, a feminist organization, debunked rape culture to the US Department of Justice, Everyday Feminism still propagates this myth. Shannon writes,

> *"Mothers who blame girls for posting sexy selfies and leading their sons into sin, instead of talking with their sons about their responsibility for their own sexual expression."*

She cites this as an example of rape culture. However, the reverse is actually true. Mothers who express concern over their over-sexualized children are just being good parents. As we saw from previous chapters, it's the feminist sexual liberation movement that actually created this problem, not the myth of rape culture.

Shannon's next example,

> *"Calling college students who have the courage to report their rapes liars."*

What Shannon and Everyday Feminism are missing here is that no one is saying that every accusation of rape is a lie. Nor are critics claiming that all women who claim they're raped are liars. However, as we learned from earlier chapters...a lot are.

Again, even though rape culture has been debunked, everyone's getting on the idiot bandwagon by claiming everything is rape culture. For example, Eve Ensler's article for the Huffington Post, *"The Undeniable Rape Culture of Donald Trump."*

Her entire article, written during the 2016 presidential election, is a hit piece on the current President of the United States. This effort to stall his campaign was big on accusations while being completely devoid of any facts. Then she takes her baseless accusations and says they're rape culture because...reasons.

Again, rape culture had already been debunked. Yet, we see these types of fake news articles everywhere. Feminists use the verifiably debunked myth of rape culture as an excuse to witch-hunt, wrongfully demonize, and discriminate against men and women who oppose feminist ideology.

Now if the short bus had stopped there, it might not be so bad.

It didn't.

Once called out on their hypocrisy and intellectual dishonesty, feminists didn't double down...they went full retard.

How? Allow me to describe the ways.

Man-spreading was a feminist created campaign against men who spread their legs while sitting to avoid testicle and genital discomfort. Feminists rallied and used it to discriminate against men by claiming it was sexist. However, in this case, it wasn't just the feminists who bought into this idiotic hysteria. The police bought into this stupidity. They even considered it a crime and started arresting people for it.

It became such a huge thing that the New York Transit Authority starting making anti-manspreading public service announcements for it and the New York City police were arresting men for it. However, New York wasn't alone in its discrimination against men. Other police departments around the Western world have joined the special olympics here as well.

The whole campaign discriminated against men and criminalized them for attempting to ease their discomfort...something man-hating feminists see as a crime.

Yet, man-spreading wasn't the only discriminatory campaign against men, there were many others after it. This included, but wasn't limited to, the idiotic "sexist office temperature" campaign. In fact, feminists started shitting out idiotic and bigoted campaigns so quickly, they took a life of their own.

They became the social justice movement.

The social justice campaign decided to merge many loosely organized movements under the "social justice" umbrella. This included the lesbian movement, the gay movement, the debunked transgender movement, and the ever-growing, intersectional feminist movement.

The intersectional feminist movement backfired a bit because it divided feminists by race, creed, age, geopolitical affiliation, national origin and anything else that seems convenient. So thanks to intersectional feminism, you have new feminist sub-movements. There were: African-American feminists, Latina feminists, Asian feminists, Native American feminists, disabled feminists, transgender feminists, and more are being created every day. I'd be surprised if there isn't a Kekistani feminist movement formed within the next year.

The best part, their internal divisions inadvertently created a victimocracy and an oppression olympics that started infighting to decide who was the most oppressed. Hilariously, they're still cannibalizing themselves today.

What they failed to realize is that if everyone's oppressed, no one is.

The members of this campaign unironically called themselves social justice warriors (SJWs). However, one look at their membership, in its entirety, and it's clear to see that the social justice movement is primarily a self-segregated insane asylum.

In fact, social justice warriors are so ill-equipped to defend their ideologies, they often refuse to openly or publicly debate those who disagree with them. This refusal is born out of a sense of self-preservation.

You see, when SJWs are demonstratively proven wrong, they don't concede, they throw a tantrum. As many YouTube videos show, this is bad for marketing and optics. There are videos all over the internet of SJWs having mental breakdowns when confronted by those who disagree with them. Sadly, these mental breakdowns can occur even if the person who disagrees isn't actually in their presence; an image on a video screen is enough to send them into fits.

Pavlov would be proud.

At some point, SJWs figured out this might not be perceived as positive.

However, rather than change their ideological world view to fit the facts, they decided to suppress them instead. This was accomplished through protest. The more rational of their group, including prominent and well-established feminists, would start an intimidation campaign through a combination of writing letters and publicly speaking out against any organization that allowed anyone who opposed SJW bigotry a platform to speak. At the same time, the more autistic SJWs and those more prone to fits would protest in the streets and at any event where opposing opinions might be given. Then, if rational people who disagreed with SJW bigotry showed up to the events, the SJW protests would often deteriorate into violence...usually started by the SJWs themselves.

However, their bigotry didn't end there.

I was serious when I said they went full retard.

In the 1950s-1960s, civil rights leaders protested bigotry they saw around them. Blacks were subjected to segregation laws, interracial marriage was considered a crime, and there were laws that limited blacks access, even to public spaces like busses. They were even excluded from public schools, colleges, and institutions. Their voices were effectively silenced.

In response, the original civil rights leaders and the movements that surrounded them protested to protect freedom of speech, stop segregation, and to stop racially motivated violence and bigotry. Overall, these protests were successful.

Fast forward to 2017. The current social justice movement stands for none of these things. They've advocated for segregation in the form of safe spaces. SJWs have spoken in favor of and inspired their followers to commit many hate crimes against whites and others who are perceived as having ideological differences. Finally, they've actively opposed free speech. In the 1960s, Berkeley marched to protest in favor of free speech. In 2017, SJWs marched in protest opposing free speech. Even committing well-documented violence against free speech advocates.

Martin Luther King Jr. and Malcolm X would be turning in their graves.

Today, social justice warriors and their feminist masters

have labeled opposing views as hate speech and relentlessly attack it when they find it. Speaking out against either feminism or social justice warrior bigotry has gotten people fired from their jobs, falsely arrested, and targeted for hate crimes and harassment

However, throughout all this outrage, most people have ignored the true gravity of the problem. Feminism controls almost all Western governments and legal systems. It's firmly embedded in education at all levels, from kindergarten to post-secondary colleges and institutions.

Children aren't being taught equality...they're being indoctrinated to hate men.

Even though the transgender theory has been thoroughly debunked by biology, it's still being taught to our children, on an institutional scale. Ian Miles Cheong penned an April 23, 2017, article for Heat Street, *"Australian Govt Booklet Tells 'Gender Diverse' Teens to Consider Sex Change Surgery."* Cheong reports,

> *"The state government of Victoria in Australia had funded the production of a guide encouraging...teenagers to undergo hormone therapy and sex reassignment surgery."*
>
> *The following month, Amanda Prestigiacomo reported in the Daily Wire article, "Australian Schools say They'll Facilitate Gender Changes for 6 Year-Olds" that,*
>
> *"Nearly 300 schools in Victoria, Australia, have signed on to new transgender policy guidelines which would allow schools to facilitate the gender transition of students as*

> *young as six years of age without so much as parental consent."*

Like I said...indoctrinated. This is so concerning that the American College of Pediatricians on January 2017, released the following statement,

> *"The American College of Pediatricians urges healthcare professionals, educators and legislators to reject all policies that condition children to accept as normal a life of chemical and surgical impersonation of the opposite sex.*
>
> *Facts – not ideology – determine reality.*
>
> *Human sexuality is an objective biological binary trait: "XY" and "XX" are genetic markers of male and female, respectively – not genetic markers of a disorder. The norm for human design is to be conceived either male or female. Human sexuality is binary by design with the obvious purpose being the reproduction and flourishing of our species. This principle is self-evident. The exceedingly rare disorders of sex development (DSDs), including but not limited to testicular feminization and congenital adrenal hyperplasia, are all medically identifiable deviations from the sexual binary norm, and are rightly recognized as disorders of human design.*
>
> *No one is born with a gender. Everyone is born with a biological sex.*
>
> *Gender (an awareness and sense of oneself as male or female) is a sociological and psychological concept; not an objective*

> *biological one. No one is born with an awareness of themselves as male or female; this awareness develops over time and, like all developmental processes, may be derailed by a child's subjective perceptions, relationships, and adverse experiences from infancy forward. People who identify as "feeling like the opposite sex" or "somewhere in between" do not comprise a third sex. They remain biological men or biological women.*
>
> *A person's belief that he or she is something they are not is, at best, a sign of confused thinking. When an otherwise healthy biological boy believes he is a girl, or an otherwise healthy biological girl believes she is a boy, an objective psychological problem exists that lies in the mind not the body, and it should be treated as such."*

Further, these types of programs are coming to the United States, with more leftist strongholds already implementing them in some form in our children's schools.

Even worse, the feminist created social justice movement is actively testing the waters to try to get society's endorsement of child sex abuse, otherwise known as pedophilia.

In 2015, the Left was so interested in normalizing child rape, it allowed self-admitted pedophile, Todd Nickerson, a platform to pen the article, *"I'm a Pedophile, but not a Monster,"* on Salon.com. Nickerson tries to write a persuasive essay on the reasons you should be accepting of pedophilia.

Two years later, pedophiles are trying to rebrand

themselves as pedosexuals and want to change the LBGT+ tag to LBGTP+ tag to show support for pedophiles. They even have a hashtag for twitter, #pedosexual.

Yes, I'm 100% serious. Even worse, they created a pro-child abuse organization called the Heart Progress Foundation which even has its own twitter hashtag: #heartprogress. Their website nickmartinezofficial.com even appropriates the Lady Gaga song lyric, *"Baby, I was born this way..."*

Further, On March 28, 2017, pedophile Nick Martinez writes wrote a blog post on their official website entitled, *"Heart Progress Foundation: A Growing Era of Tolerance."* In it he states,

> *"In my journey of embracing the left and joining groups of other like minded individuals, I stumbled upon a group known as Heart Progress Foundation. Heart Progress Foundation is a revolutionary new group that is seeking to spread awareness of the plight of pedosexuals.*
>
> *Founded by Ernst Steiner, himself an advocate for people with pedosexuality in 2016, it has gained much momentum and is growing daily in membership.*
>
> *Much like the LGBT movements of the past, the pedosexual movement is beginning to take off and fight for its equality. We, the people, whether we are gay, bi, lesbian, straight, white, black, Latino, Asian, or pedosexual are part of the new era of acceptance and tolerance."*

You read it correctly. It's a pro-child molester group

where they can network together.

It's growing daily.

Prior to that, the American Psychological Association (APA) publicly classified pedophilia as a sexual orientation in its DSM-5, the Diagnostic and Statistical Manual of Mental Disorders released in May 2013. However, after it was discovered by an independent journalist and reported on, the backlash was so massive that the APA backtracked and promised to change the designation. To save face, they claimed it was an "oversight."

In the 2016 election, feminist and self-admitted pedophile Lena Dunham was allowed to interview the Democratic candidate for President Hillary Clinton. Why do I call Dunham a pedophile? It's because in Dunham's memoir, *"Not that Kind of Girl"* she confesses to grooming her sister,

> *"As she grew, I took to bribing her for her time and affection: one dollar in quarters if I could do her makeup like a "motorcycle chick." Three pieces of candy if I could kiss her on the lips for five seconds. Whatever she wanted to watch on TV if she would just "relax on me." Basically, anything a sexual predator might do to woo a small suburban girl I was trying."*

She goes on in another passage,

> *"I shared a bed with my sister...until I was seventeen years old. She was afraid to sleep alone and would begin asking me around 5:00 P.M. every day whether she could sleep with me. I put on a big show of saying no, taking pleasure in watching her beg and*

> *sulk, but eventually I always relented. Her sticky, muscly little body thrashed beside me every night as I read Anne Sexton, watched reruns of SNL, sometimes even as I slipped my hand into my underwear to figure some stuff out."*

Since Dunham's memoir was released in late 2015, the DNC and the Clinton campaign knew or should have known Dunham was a confessed pedophile before their interview...but clearly that didn't matter. Allowing a pedophile to interview Clinton on national TV, to me, constitutes an endorsement of child abuse.

Do you want some feminist or SJW ideologue brainwashing your children into thinking that child sex abuse or transgender indoctrination is ok?

The Indoctrination that misinforms our children on things as basic as science and promotes pedophilia is not only unhealthy, it's unethical. This is especially true for efforts attempting to normalize child sex abuse.

It's clear that Western society is being indoctrinated in feminist ideology on a scale that would make the founders of the Hitler Youth jealous. You see, Hitler only had ten years to create his third Reich. Feminism's had over a century.

10 THE SOLUTIONS

If you made it this far and you're against feminism, I have some bad news for you.

Feminism controls all Western governments and influences all court systems. Many feminists aren't only attorneys, they're also judges presiding over cases. In the medical field, feminists make up the vast majority of nurses and female doctors. Feminists entirely control the educational system.

Feminism won.

The reality is that for people who oppose feminism like you and me, we aren't the opposition...we're the resistance. Feminism has become like the Sith Empire from Star Wars. Its Darth Sidious is Gloria Steinem. As a side note, if you've seen a recent picture of Steinem, just imagine her in a black hood and robes. She even resembles Sidious.

The good news is that men are starting to wake up to the

threat of feminism. In countries truly dominated by feminism, the birth rate is falling, the marriage rate is falling, and women are complaining because smart men won't even commit to being their boyfriends, let alone their husbands.

Why? It's because men are tired of being constantly the targets of false rape and DV allegations.

Now, I'm not talking about the men who're cucks and manginas who still buy into the lies about feminism. I'm specifically referring to the men whose penis doesn't live in a purse and whose spine isn't on layaway, you know, the red-pilled men.

How do we solve this problem? In the short-term, there are only a few solutions that I can perceive.

We need to stand against censorship and continue to speak out against the feminist lies as we find them. However, when opposing feminism online, we should strongly consider using anonymous handles. Offline, try to use pen names for articles and be very careful. It's well documented that feminists will reframe disagreement as a hate crime and use this as justification to attempt to destroy their detractor's reputation. They've been well documented for making calls for violence against critics. They've even called for their supporters to murder their critics.

This should show the extent of both their fear and their fanaticism. Feminism functions like a cult.

These threats should never be taken lightly. If you do have to defend yourself, remember, dead enemies don't come back. Also, corpses serve as a cautionary reminder for others who didn't get the memo the first time.

THE FEMINIST LIE

Disclaimer: This message is as much for those who oppose feminism, as it is for feminists or any subordinate cucks who think they wanna pay me a visit.

It reminds me of that saying, "I came into this world screaming and covered in someone else's blood, I have no problem leaving the same way."

Moving on.

Additionally, avoid feminists where it can be helped. Don't work with them. Don't help them. Don't befriend them. Don't cohabitate with them. In general, don't engage them. Under no circumstances, give them money. If you work at a place that donates money to feminist causes, try to find a job elsewhere that doesn't. Certainly, do not become romantically involved with them or marry them.

As man, this is merely self-preservation. A false rape or DV allegation will destroy your life. It's not that every woman will falsely accuse you of rape or DV, but every woman can. If she does so, not only will she destroy your life, she will most likely suffer no consequences for it.

It seems like the women we date always tell us how abusive her ex-boyfriend, ex-husband, or baby-daddy was. Knowing this, men, if you think for a second your ex hasn't said these things about you, you're being naive.

Also, this advice is also true for manginas, cucks, and especially male feminists. They'll back-stab you faster than feminists will when possible.

Start associating with others who oppose feminism, whether online or offline. While I didn't vote for Trump, I didn't vote for Clinton either in the last election. In fact, almost 50% of all voting age adult Americans didn't vote in the 2016 election. We're not the minority as feminists would have you believe...we're the silent majority.

By associating with each other, we're strengthening our own communities and social networks. In the process, we're informing, educating, learning, and supporting each other. This will put us in a better position to overturn feminist laws and policies at all levels of government and society. It's important that we work to stop allowing feminism from continuing to intimidate people who oppose its ideology. Strengthening and growing resistance communities does this.

When you run across promiscuous feminists, remember, slut-shaming works. It's a viable tool, use it.

For those who can't openly oppose feminism, become a Kekistani and join the great meme war as a /pol/ jedi. Join online forums and use satire, sarcasm and offensive humor on feminists. They're so fanatical and devoid of humor that they'll make idiots of themselves trying to figure it out.

They have zero defense against it.

Meme warfare is the gift that keeps giving when used in the opposition of feminism. I know this sounds idiotic, but bear with me. One of the great heroes of the meme war is the /pol/ Jedi Order. They're an online forum who're the masters at coming up with fake campaigns to troll feminists and their supporters.

Examples include the famous "*Free Bleeding*" movement. /Pol/ hatched a plan to see if they could get gullible feminists avoid wearing tampons or pads during their period. They humorously claimed that feminists who allowed their period blood to flow through their clothes, for all to see, was a form of feminist activism and empowerment. Feminists bought it hook, line, and sinker.

There are images all over the internet of feminists humiliating themselves by showing off their period bloodstained clothing...some have even gone full retard with this and smeared period blood on their face. Even though it's common knowledge that /pol/ created this movement for the lulz, feminists still believe it's real. I think there's now even a clothing line sold online that displays fake blood crotch stains as a form of activism.

Then there's the *"Piss For Equality"* /pol/ campaign. In this one, /pol/ got feminists to think that being purposefully incontinent was another form of feminist empowerment and activism. They bought it and bam...Twitter feeds starting showing feminists in clothing covered in their own urine.

Then there's Pepe the Frog. This was /pol/ gold. They decided Pepe was now a racist symbol and everyone bought it. Commentators have wasted hours reporting on this fake phenomenon as though it was real. Even white supremacists bought into it and some even tried to adopt it. This troll was so convincing that the Southern Poverty Law Center bought it and wrote a piece about it being a hate symbol. Even though it's been explained to them, over and over, they still don't get it.

Then /pol/ decided the "OK" hand sign was now a symbol for white power. Social justice warriors lost their minds and started speaking out against it in large numbers.

Now when we talk about /pol/ mastery, we cannot leave out their campaign against Shia LaBeouf's *"He Will Not Divide Us"* activist art installation designed as a protest of the Trump presidency. /Pol/ was so effective at crowd-sourced research and trolling they not only destroyed this protest, when LaBeouf tried to conceal the location of the installation site, they found it in record time. By the time it ended, their efforts had caused LaBeouf to melt down, attack people, and destroy his reputation in the process. /Pol/ was so successful, they did it without a single casualty on their side. It's been explained and reported on all over the internet, check it out. It's hilarious to watch LaBeouf degenerate into autistic fits.

The /pol/ Meme Masters are legendary. They prove how gullible and humorless feminist fanatics and their followers have become. The best part, the harder the feminists and SJWs fight against the /pol/ jedi, the worse they look. Praise /pol/. Praise Kek.

Ok, so those are the potential short-term solutions. What are the long-term ones?

If you're male and you don't vote, start. Women make up 52-54% of American voters. Vote every election. Schedule your days off from work so you have election day off to make sure you vote. This is one of our strongest rights as an American citizen. If you're not voting, you're squandering it. Vote against any candidate or cause that supports feminism. Feminists get a large amount of their funding from the welfare state, through grants and other funds from the government. Your vote, when done en masse, can stop the government's feminist financing and force all those gender studies majors to go out and get a real job.

Advocate for family values. While you can do this immediately, it should be done as a long-term project. Communities that advocate for family values, overall, are safer and more civil communities. As a long-term solution, this one also addresses the problem of the sexual liberation movement and its long term consequences.

Finally, talk to like-minded people. Share your knowledge, your victories, and your failures. Through long-term community involvement, we can overcome the lies feminism continues to perpetuate.

If you read this book cover to cover, congratulations, you're now red-pilled.

Thank you for reading.

ABOUT THE AUTHOR

Bob Lewis may or may not be the author's real name. It might just be an extremely common pen name specifically employed to prevent feminists from attacking the author. The author knows that when academics, authors, documentary creators, and others speak out against the hypocrisy of feminism, they're relentlessly targeted. There are many examples of others feminists have witch-hunted in the past. To feminism, there is no greater sin than exposing the truth about their ideology.

The author spent fifteen of his first eighteen years growing up in the government foster-care system. When he was very young, he was sexually assaulted by one of his foster mothers. He was physically and emotionally abused in almost every foster home he lived in.

As an adult, he became a paralegal specializing in family law and the criminal laws associated with it. The cases he worked on were not only divorce and paternity cases, but also child dependency and parental rights termination cases. Many of the cases he worked on dealt with child abuse, sexual assault, domestic violence and often ended up in appeals courts.

He's been married and divorced twice. He was awarded custody of his children both times.

The children from his first marriage were sexually assaulted by my ex-wife's then boyfriend. Child Services knew about the child molester from an earlier case six months before he met the author's children. However, Child Services chose to hide their knowledge and did nothing when the author reported his children's abuse.

More tragically, even when presented evidence, the police also ignored it. The investigating detective was a feminist. In response, the gender-biased family court removed the children from his home and placed them with their rapist. As a result, the author's oldest son and daughter were raped and physically abused five and six days a week for five years while living in the rapist's home.

He later discovered his ex-wife knew about her children's abuse and helped hide it. After five years of relentlessly fighting the gender-biased family court system, the author eventually won and rescued his children.

His family was never the same.

Made in United States
Troutdale, OR
05/21/2025